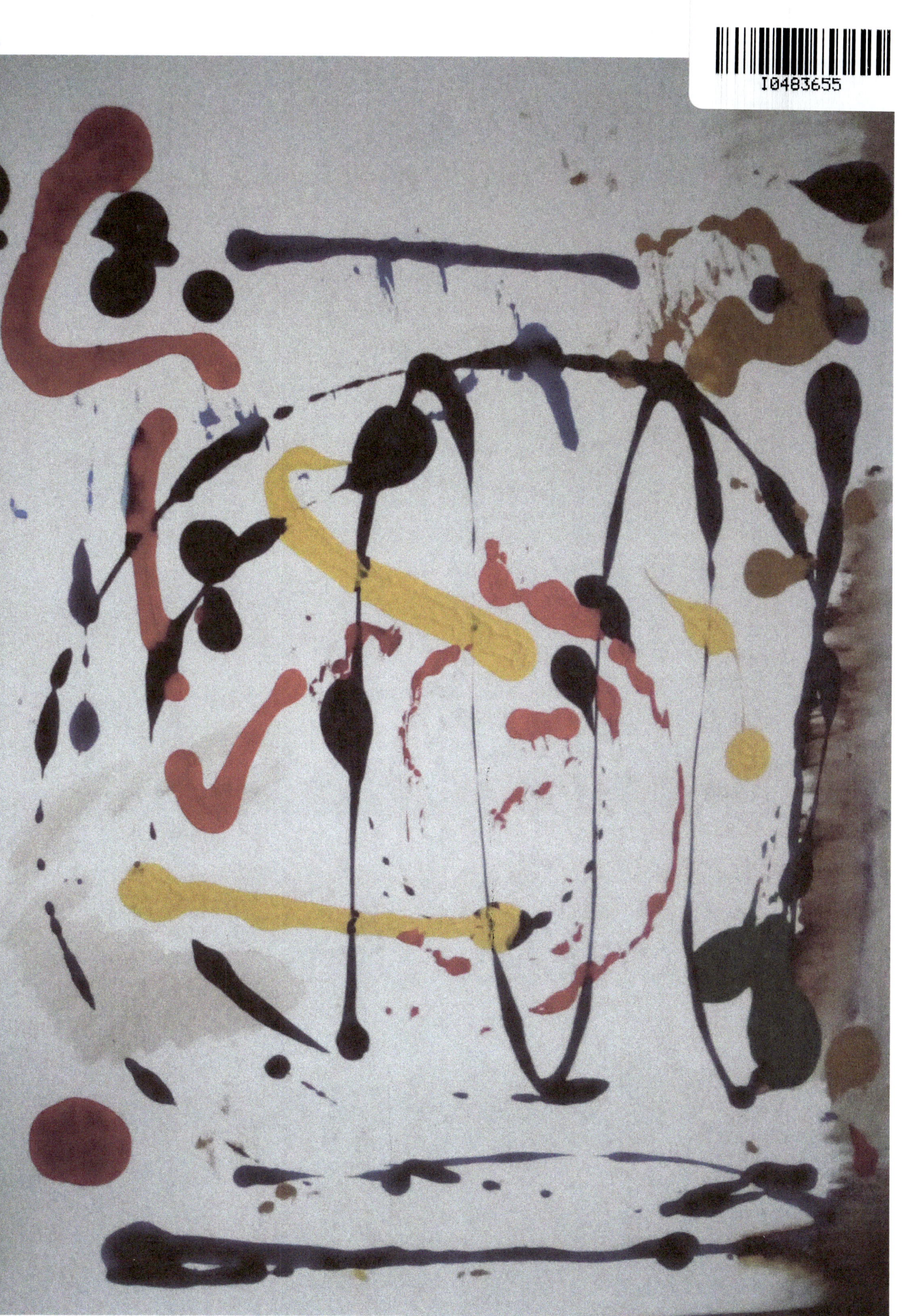

I0483655

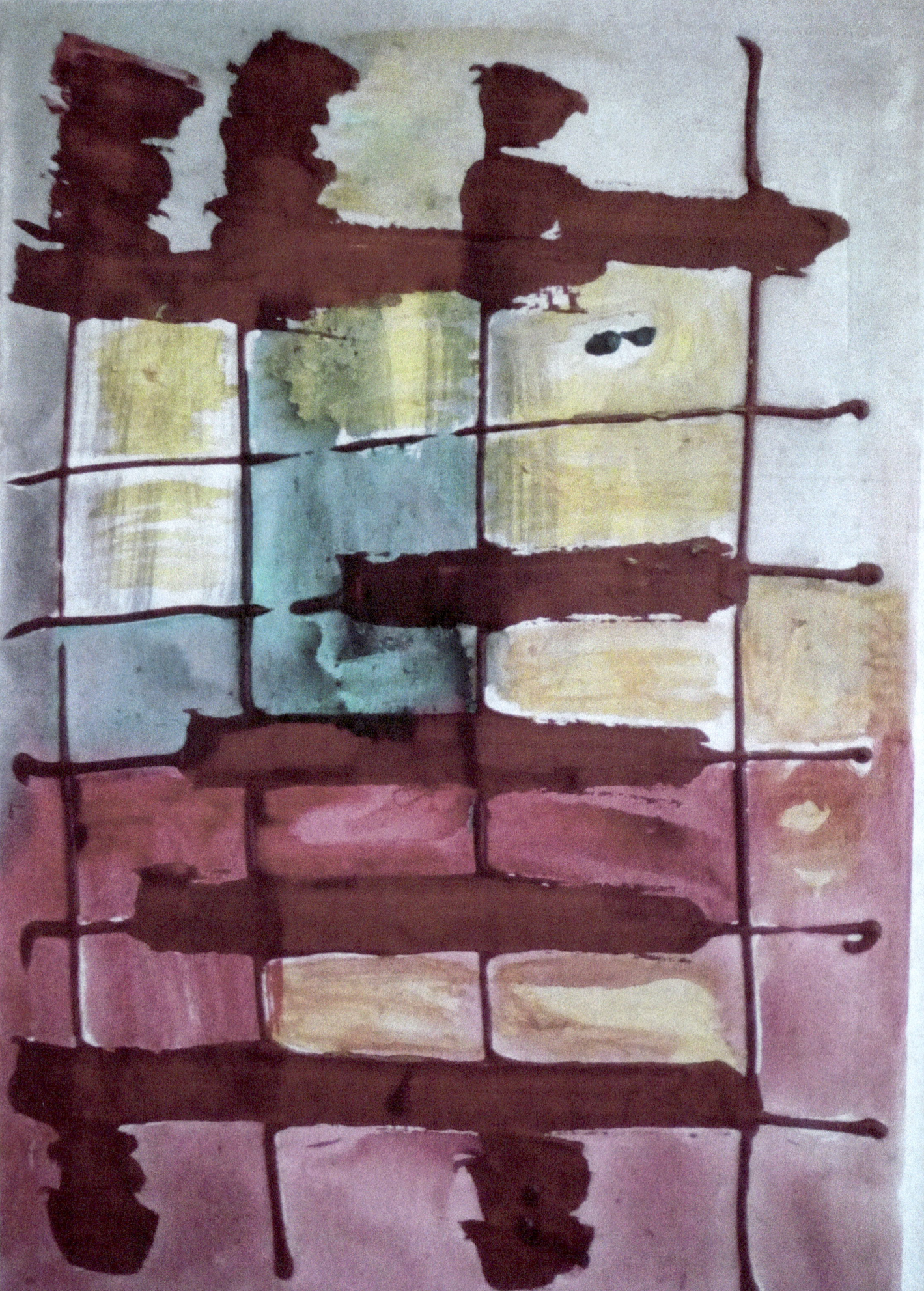

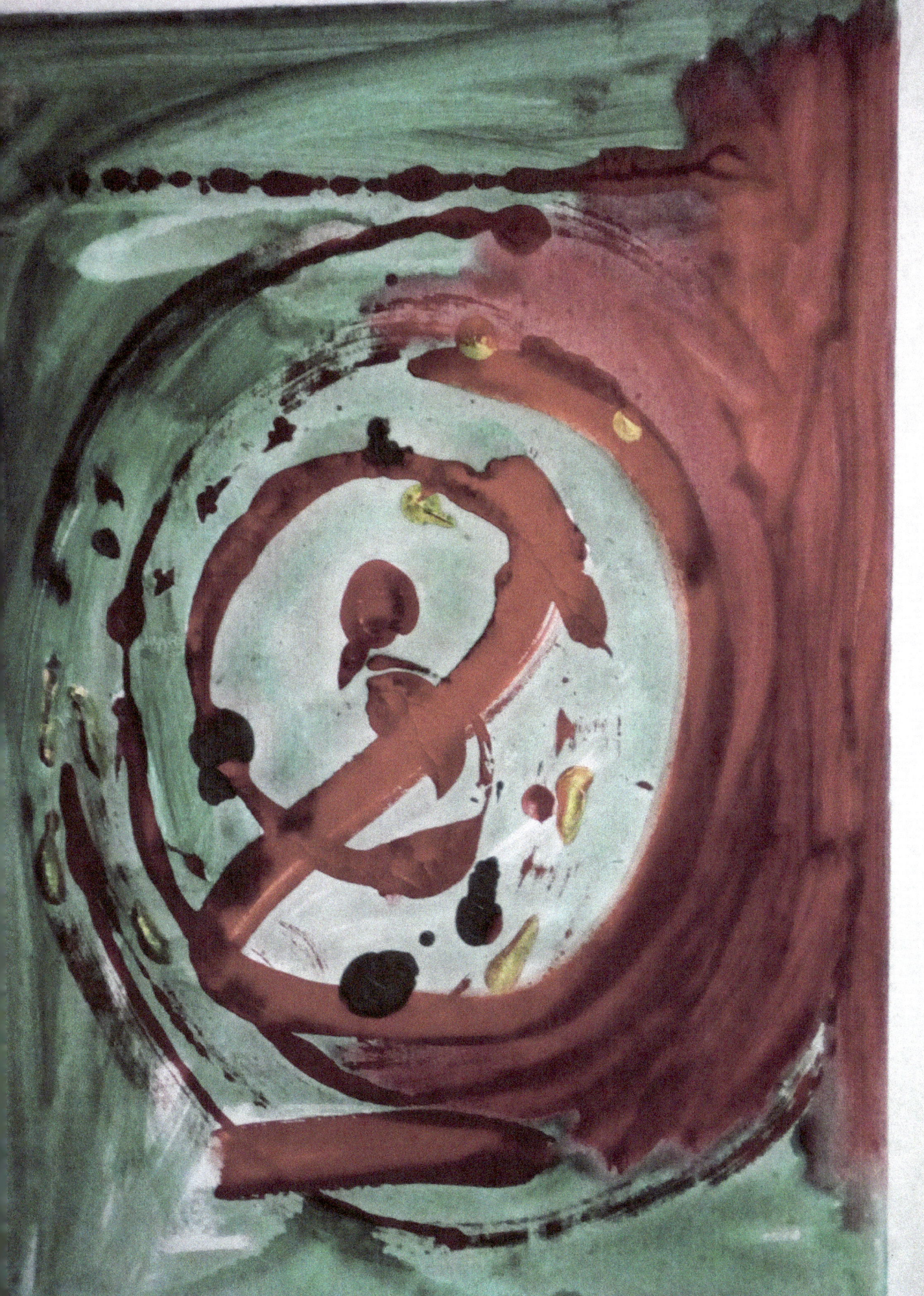

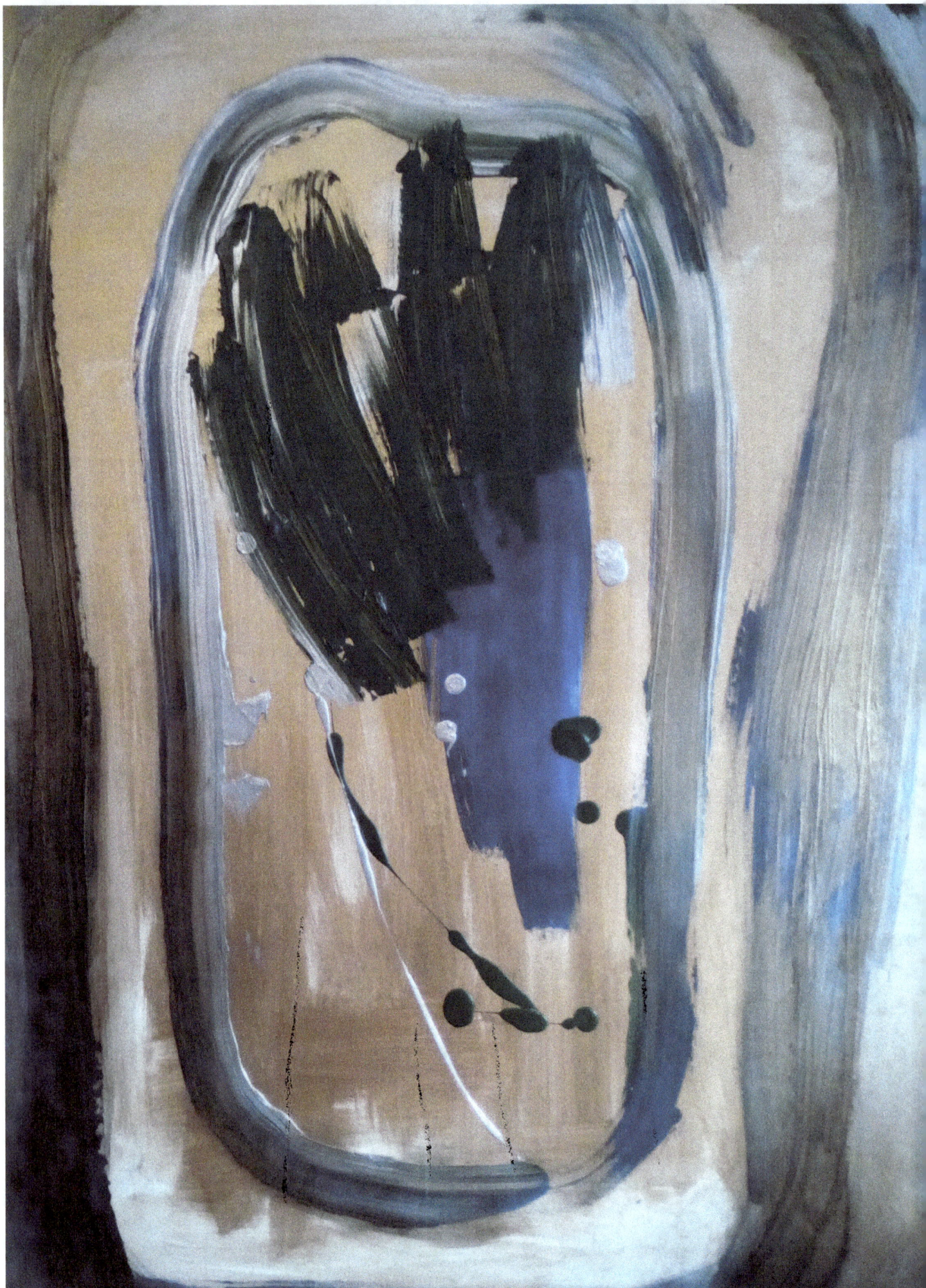

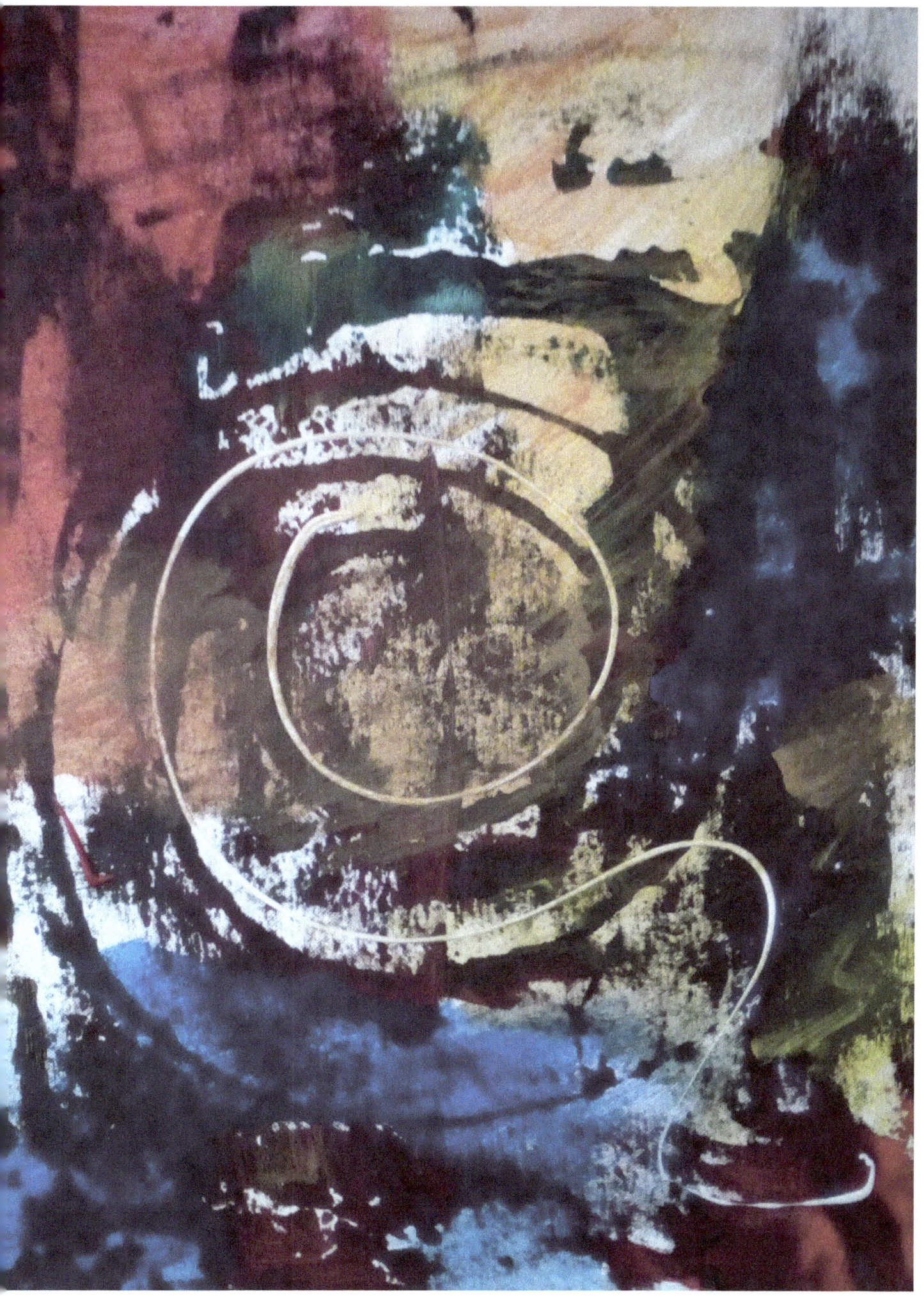

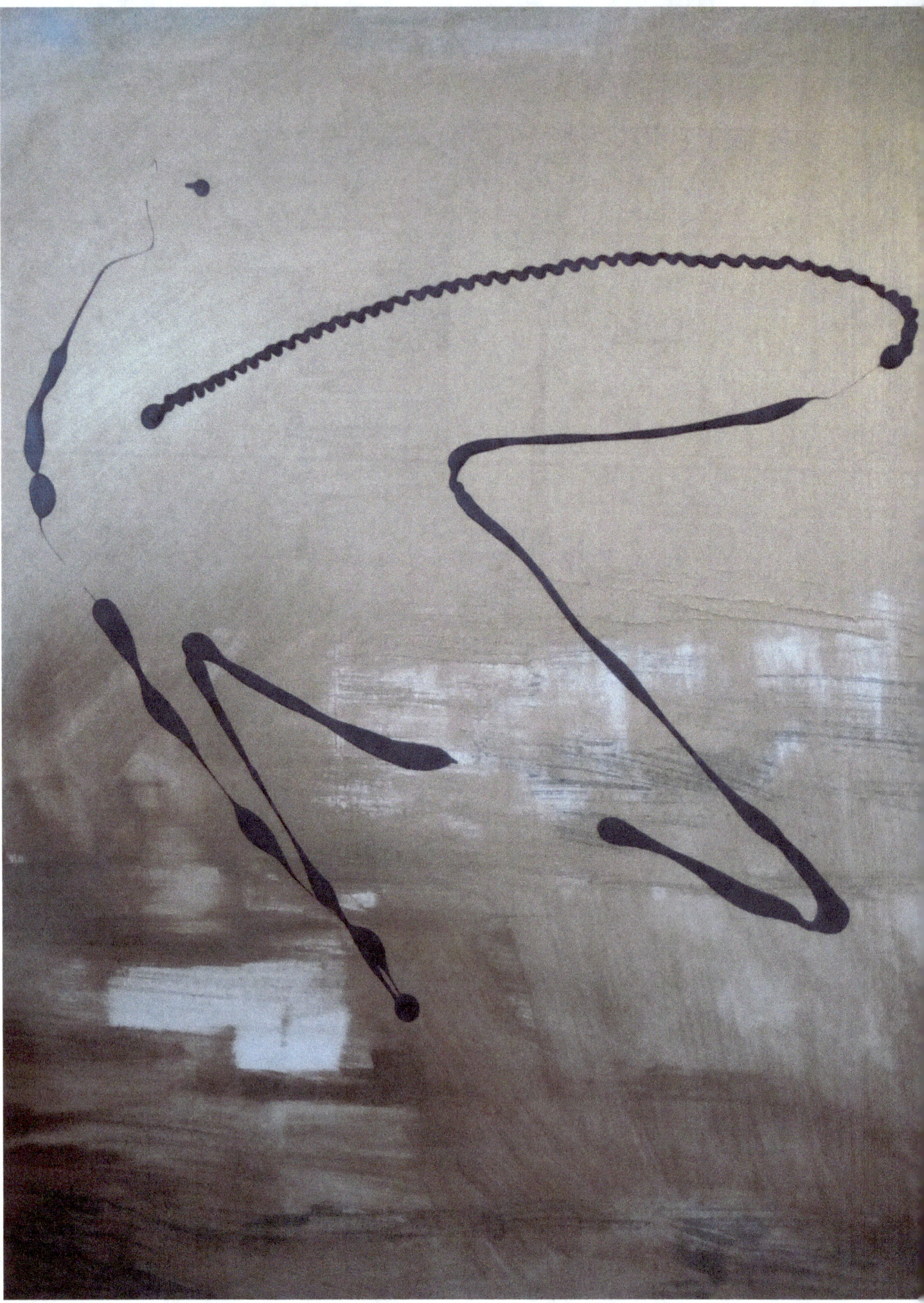

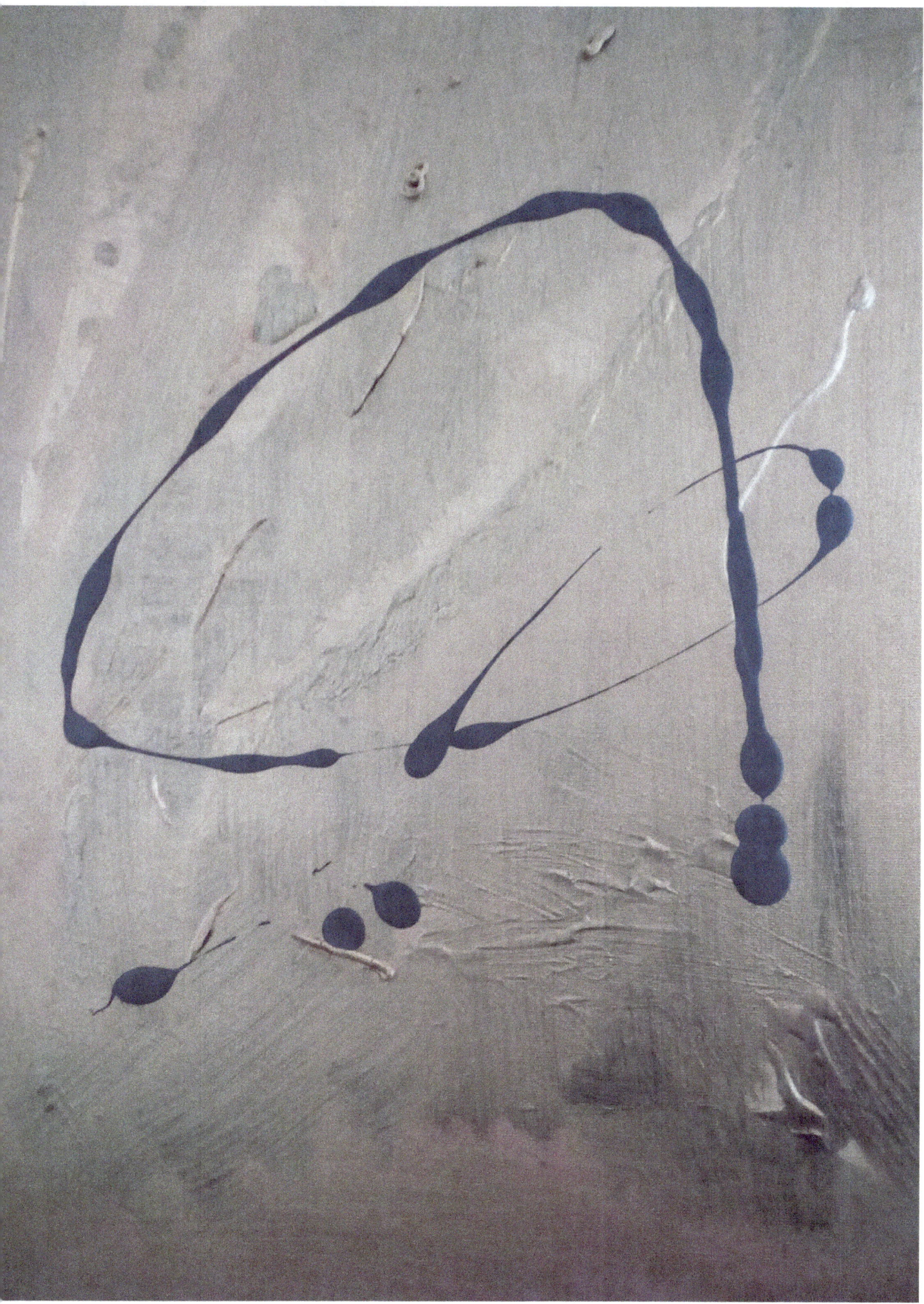

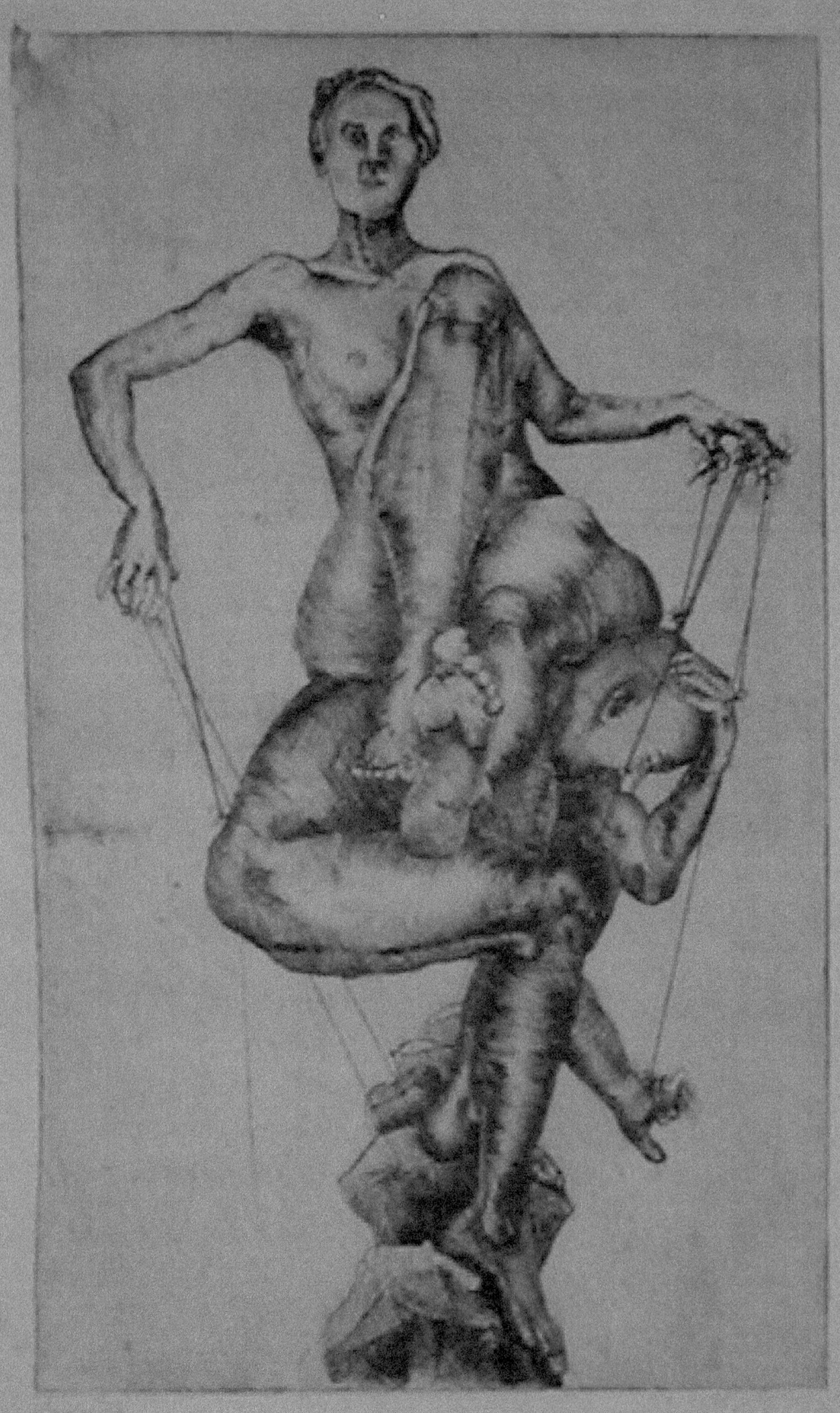

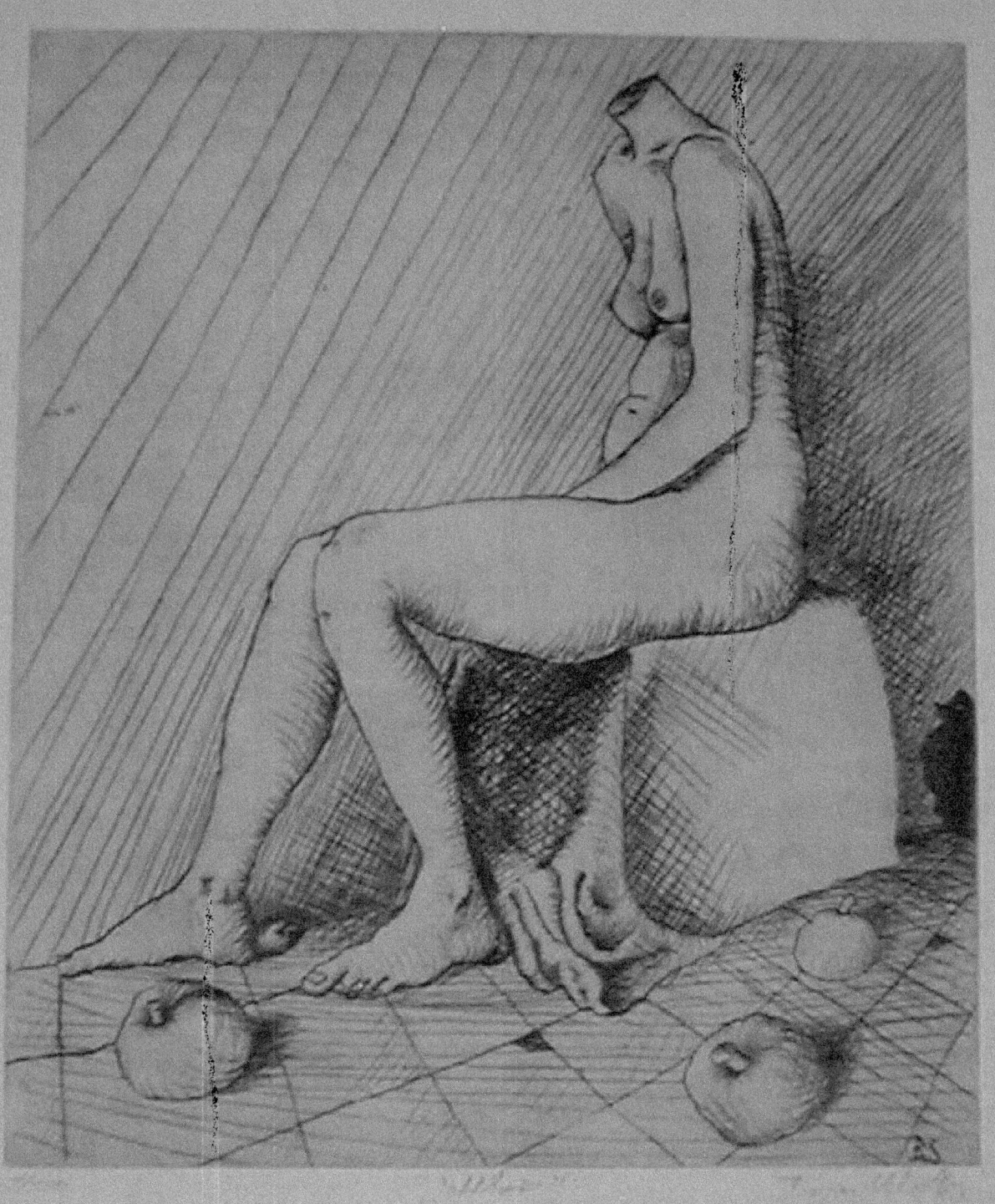

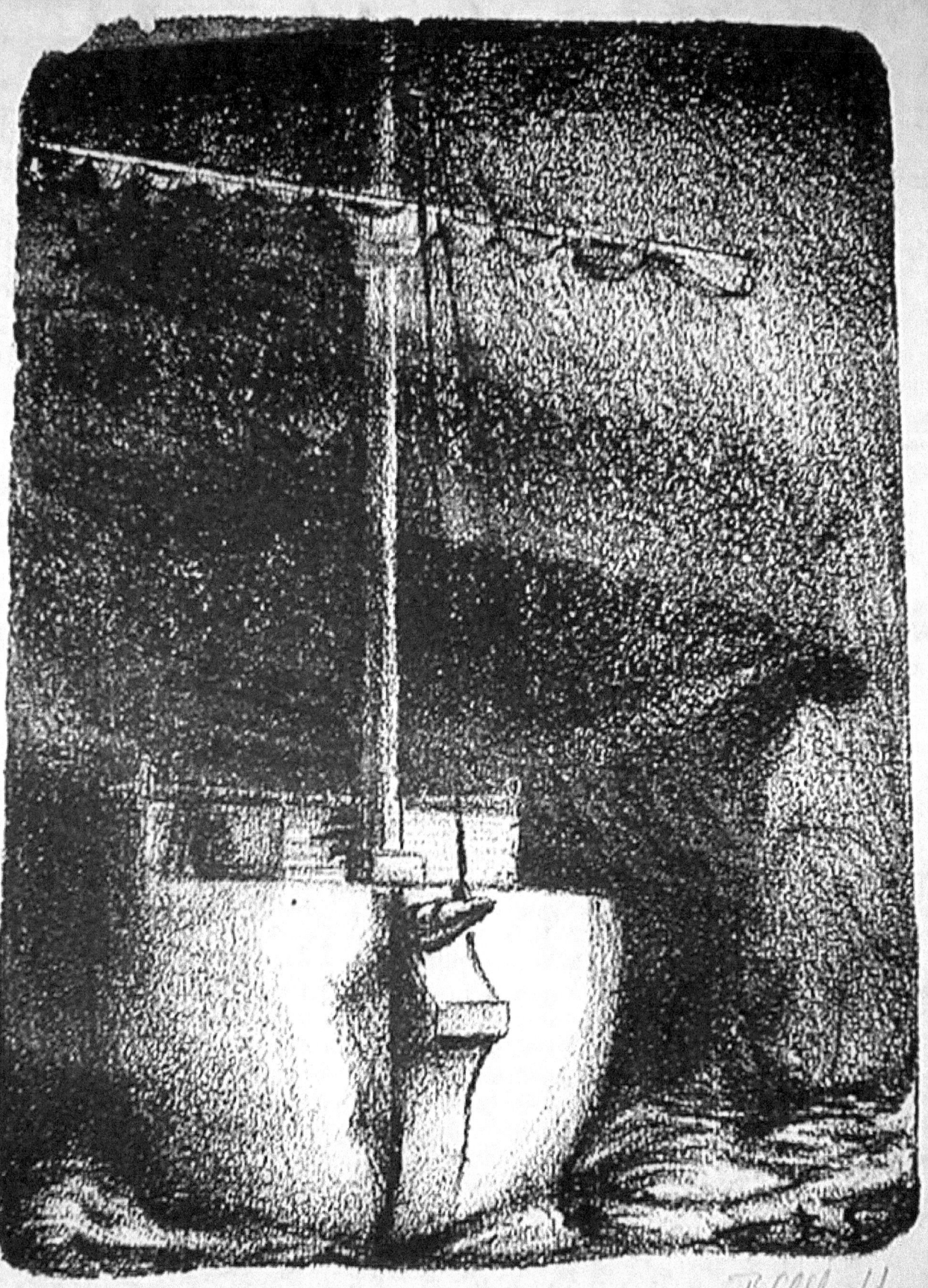

72/12   B.Clelell

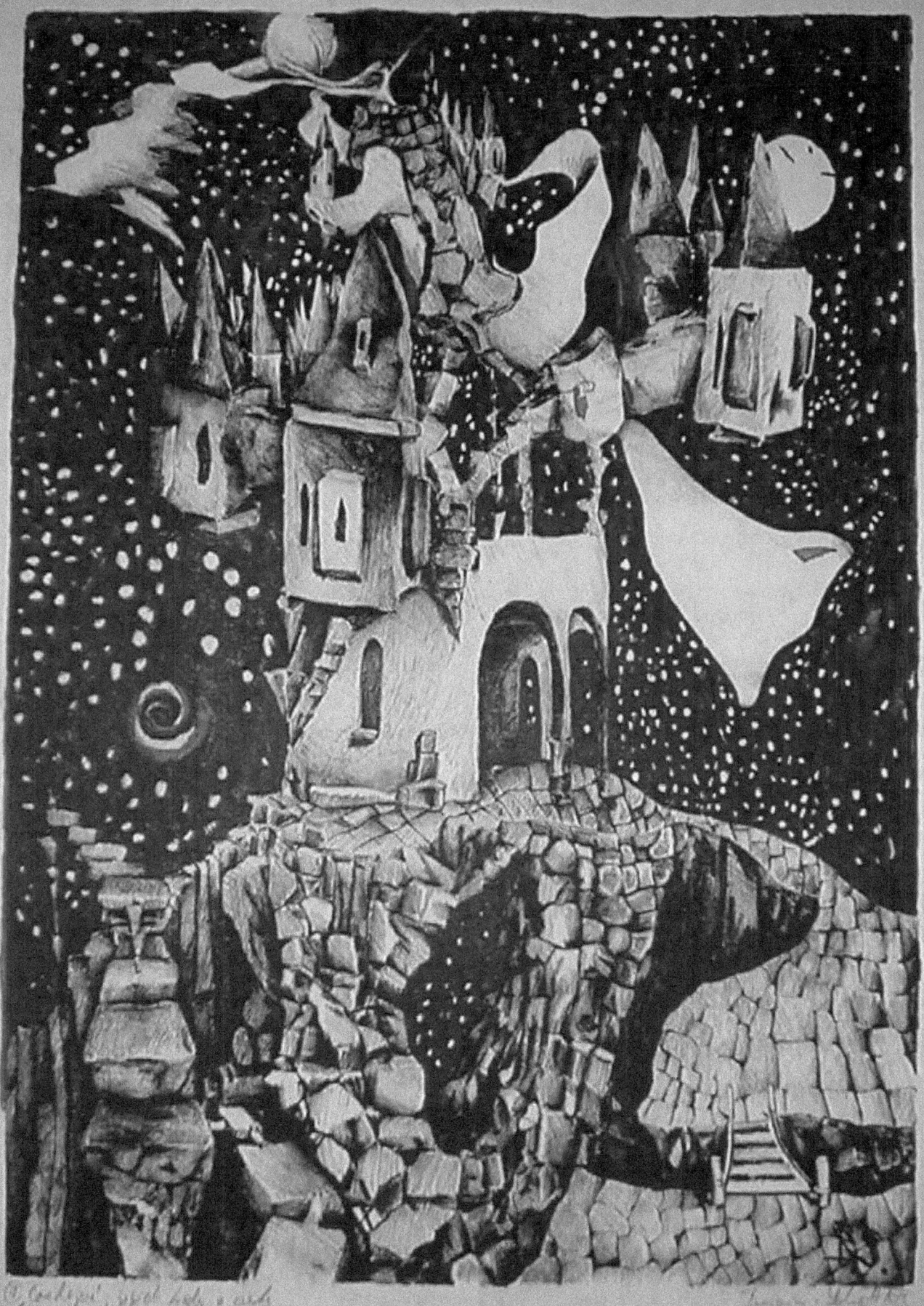

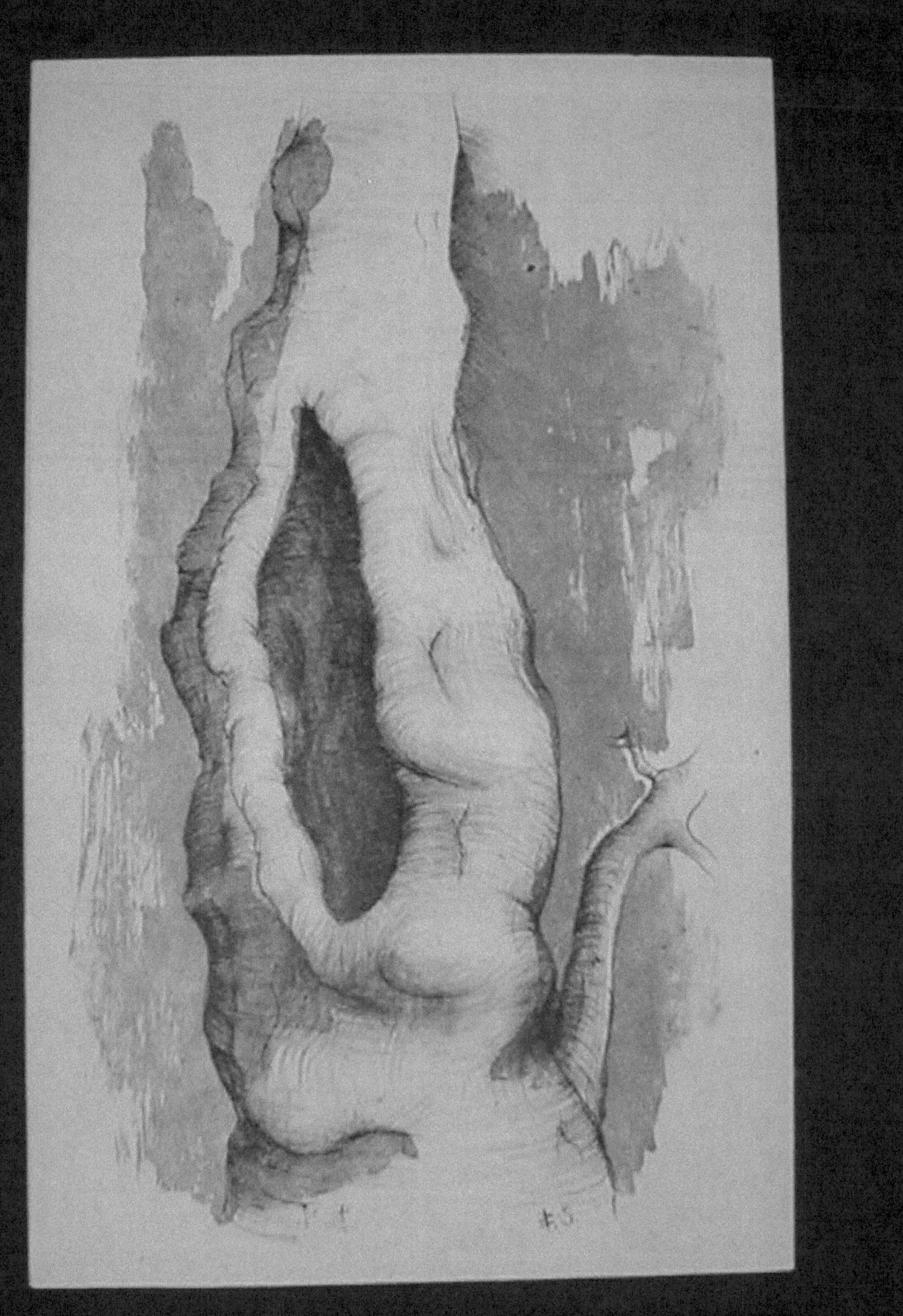

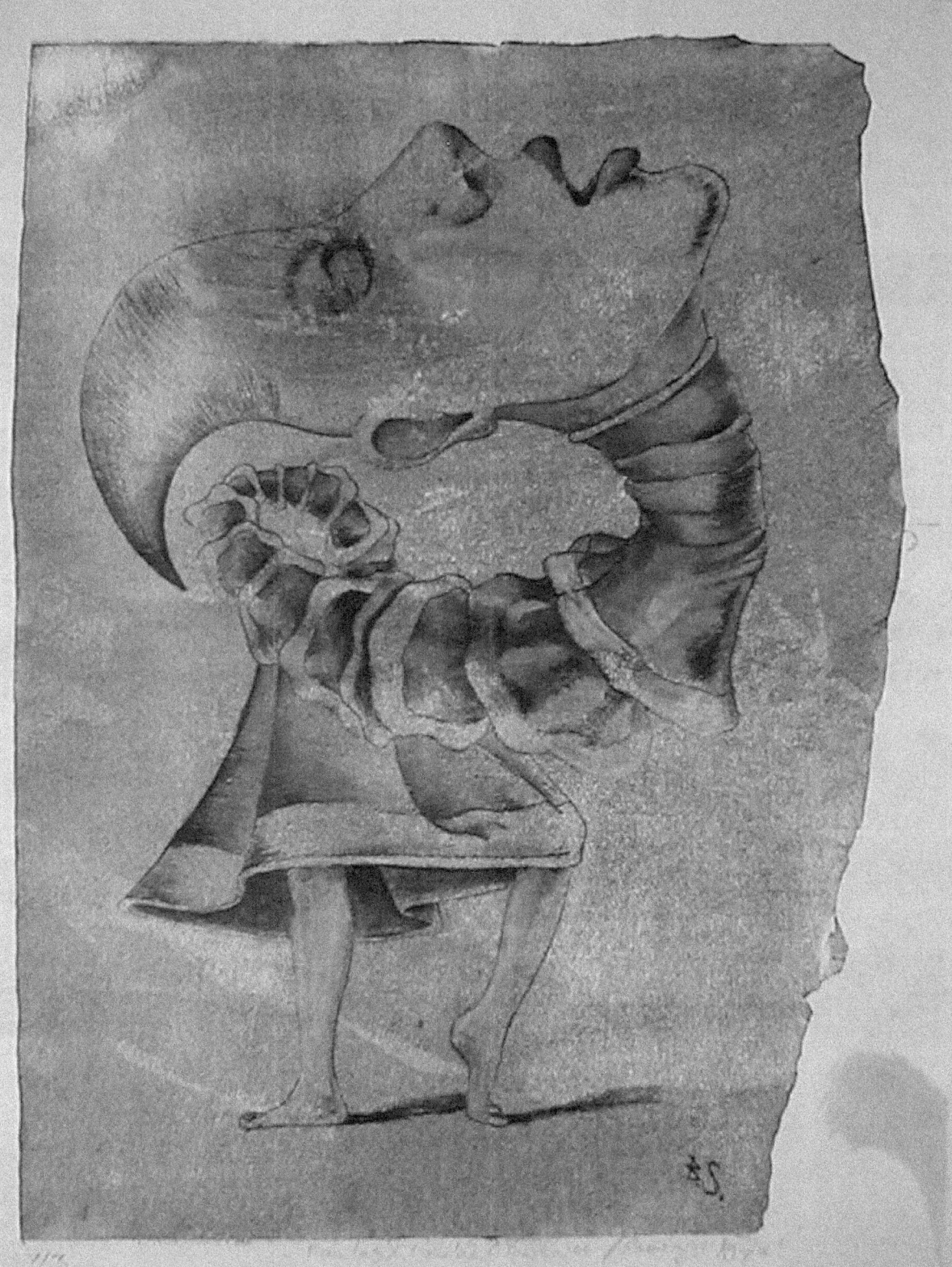

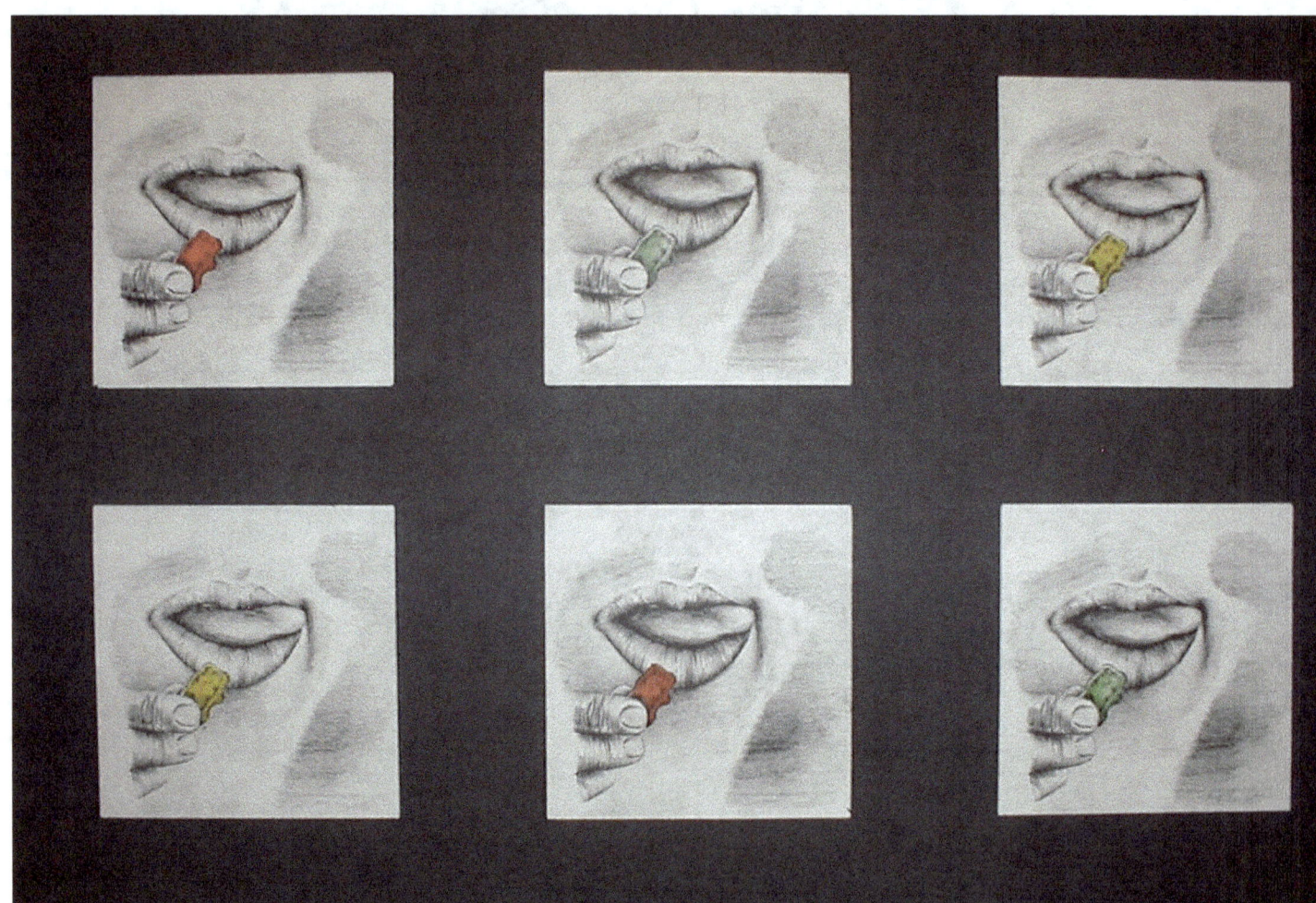

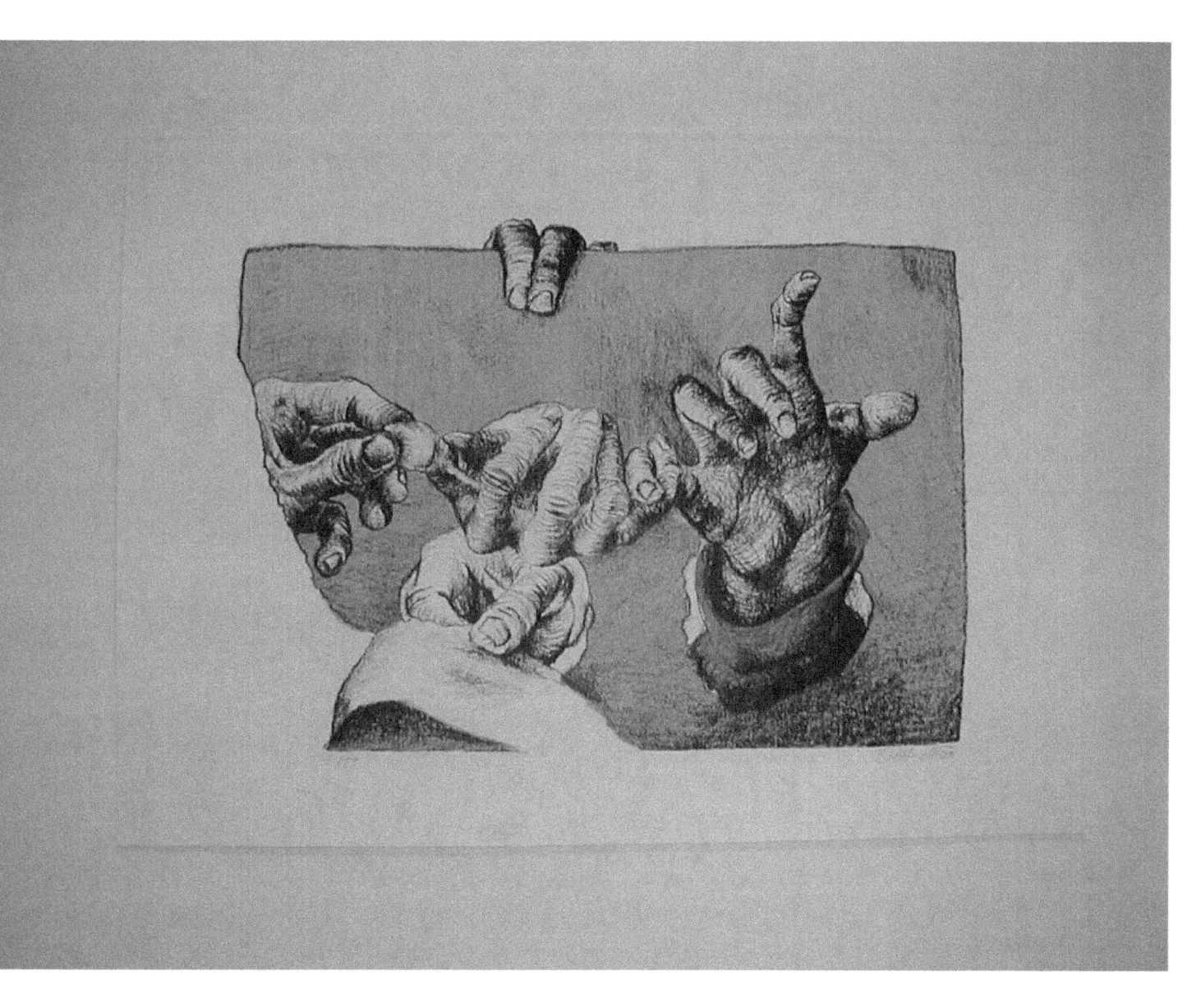

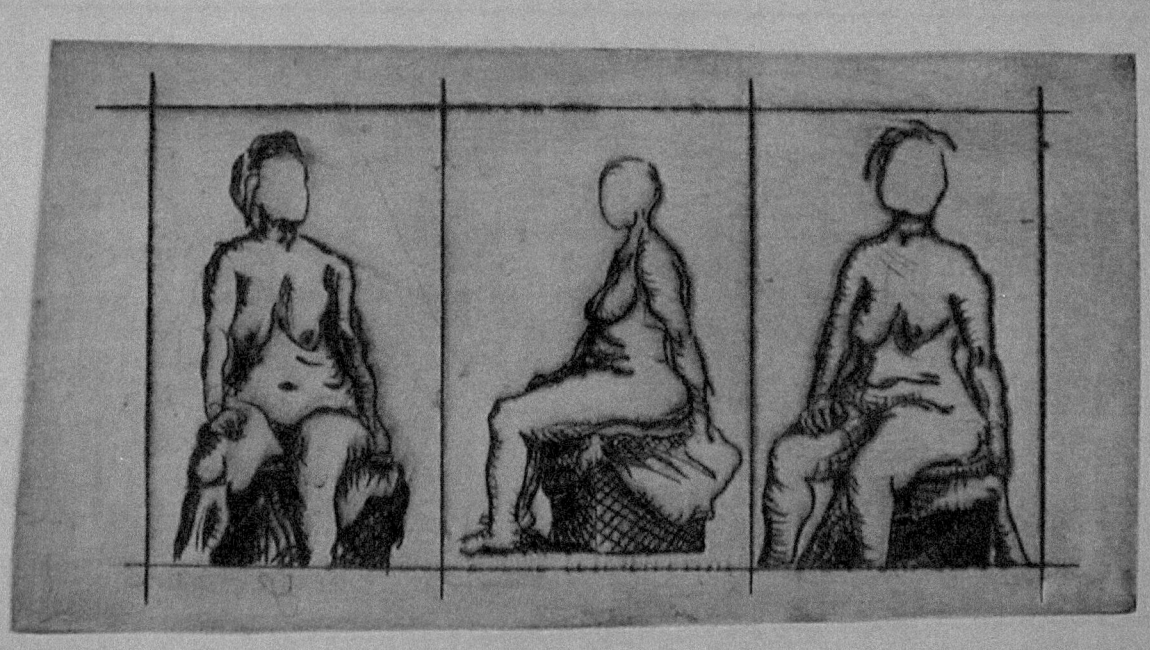

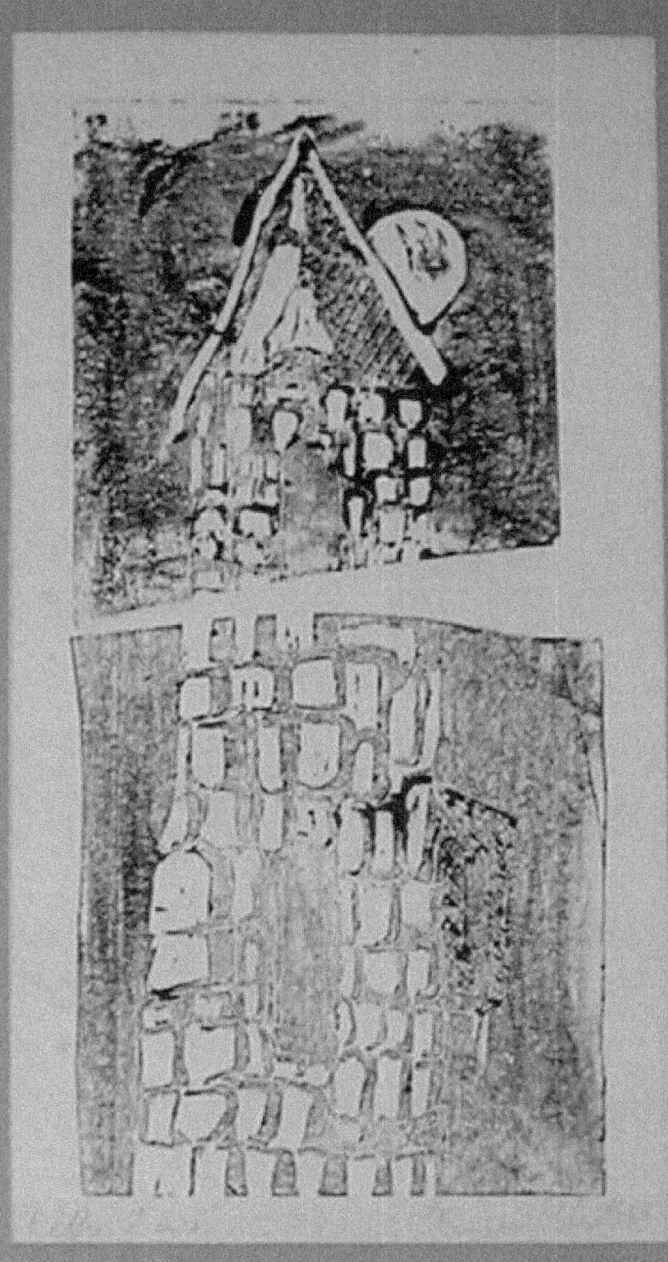

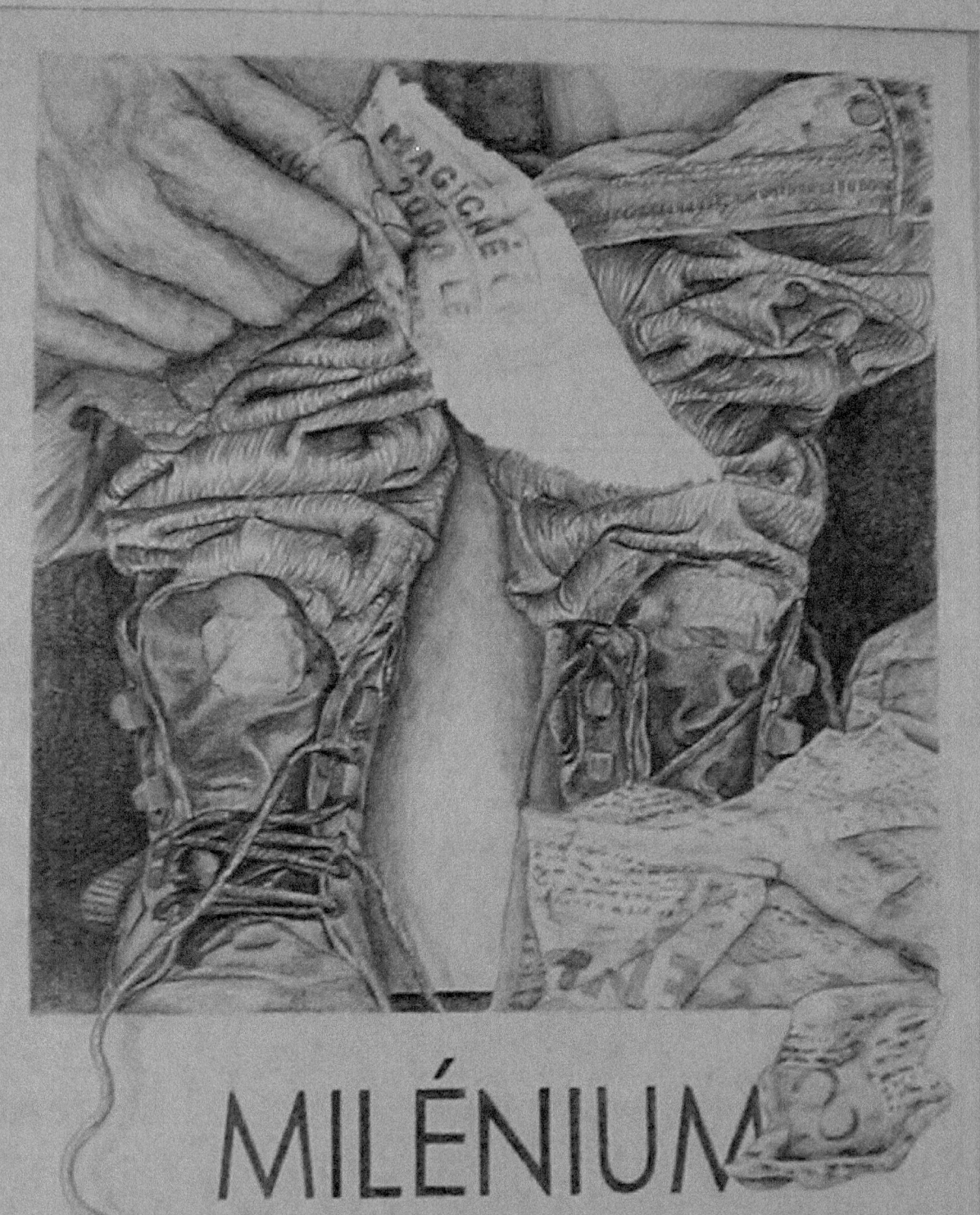

MILÉNIUM

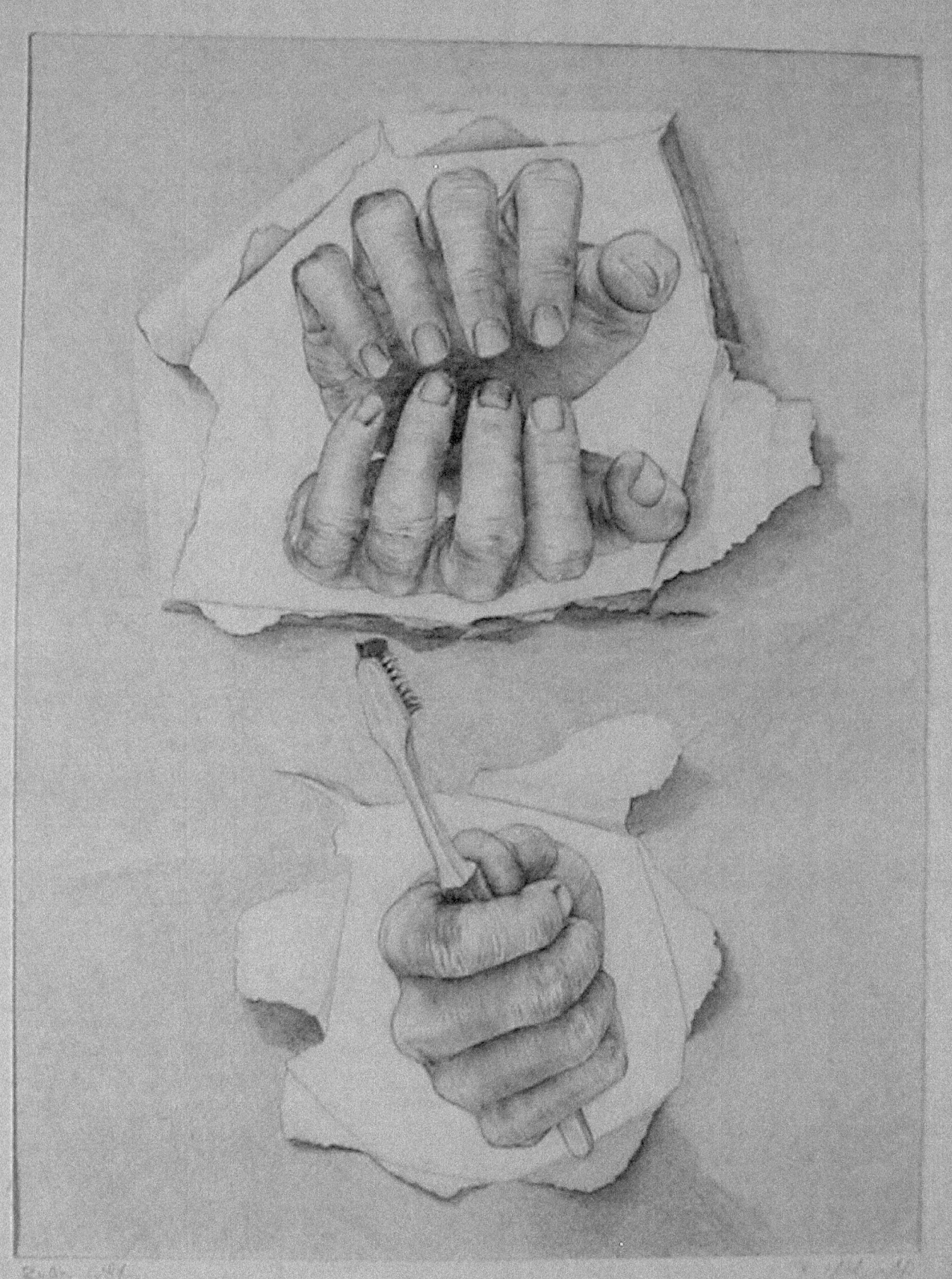

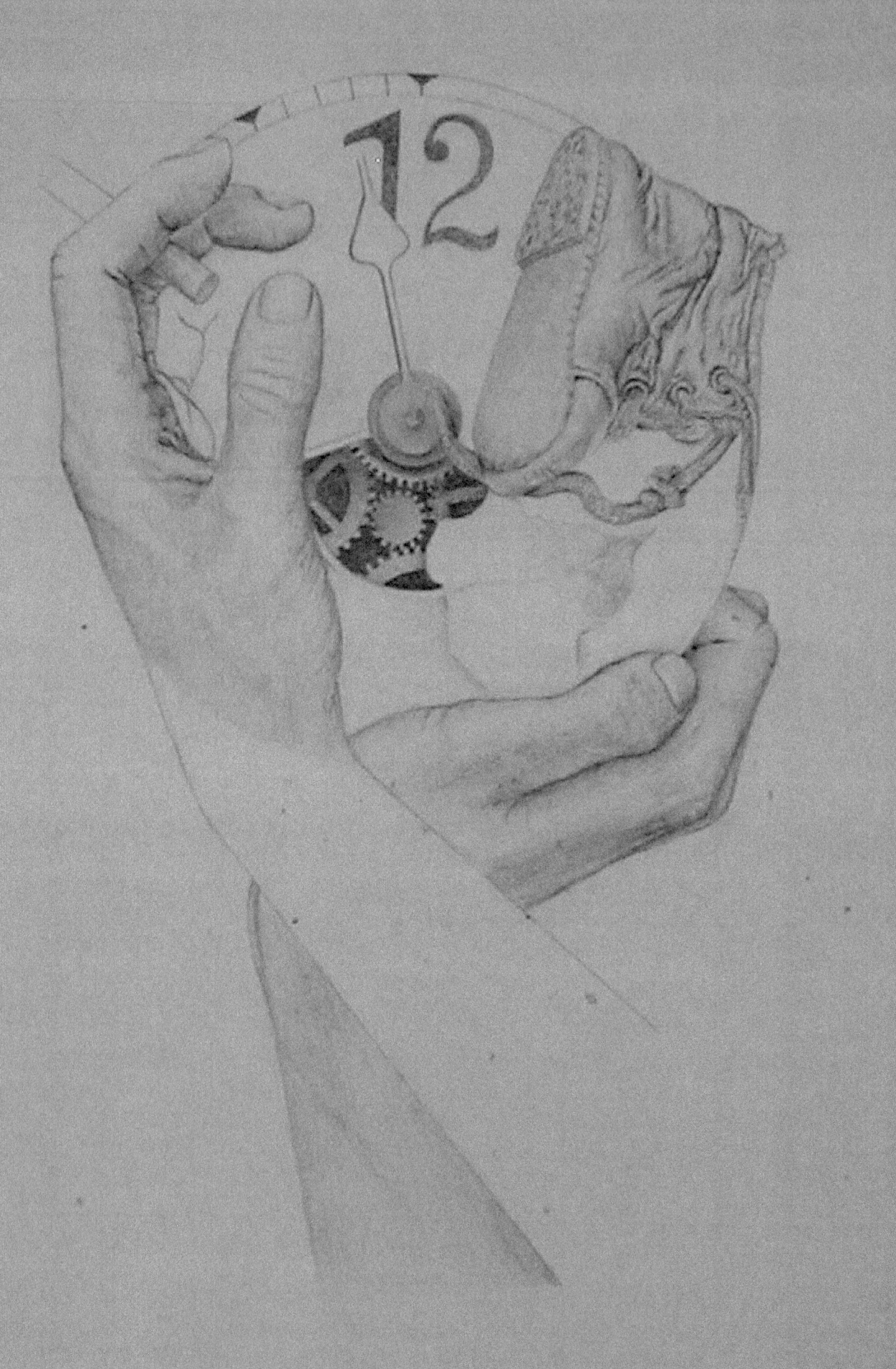

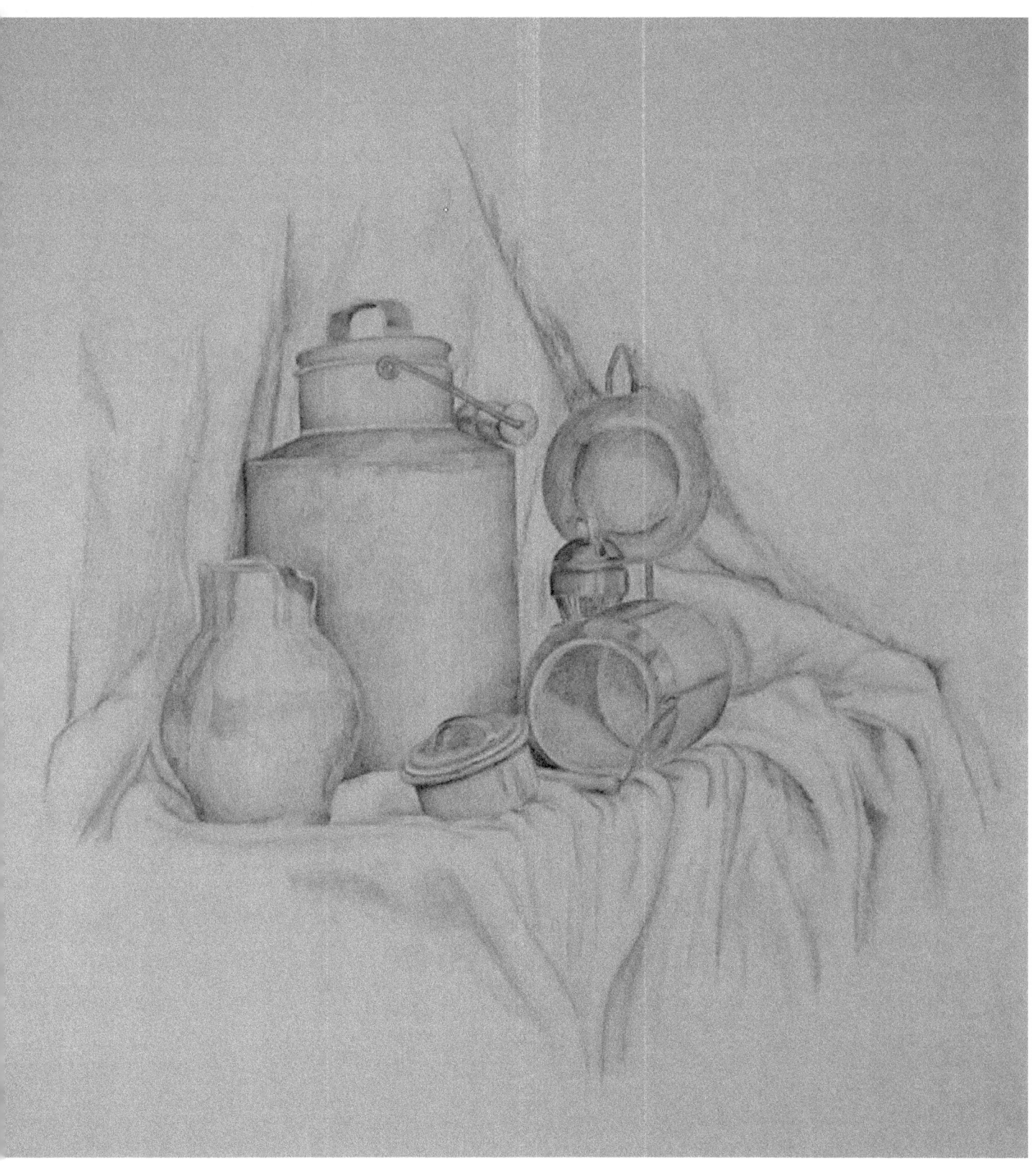

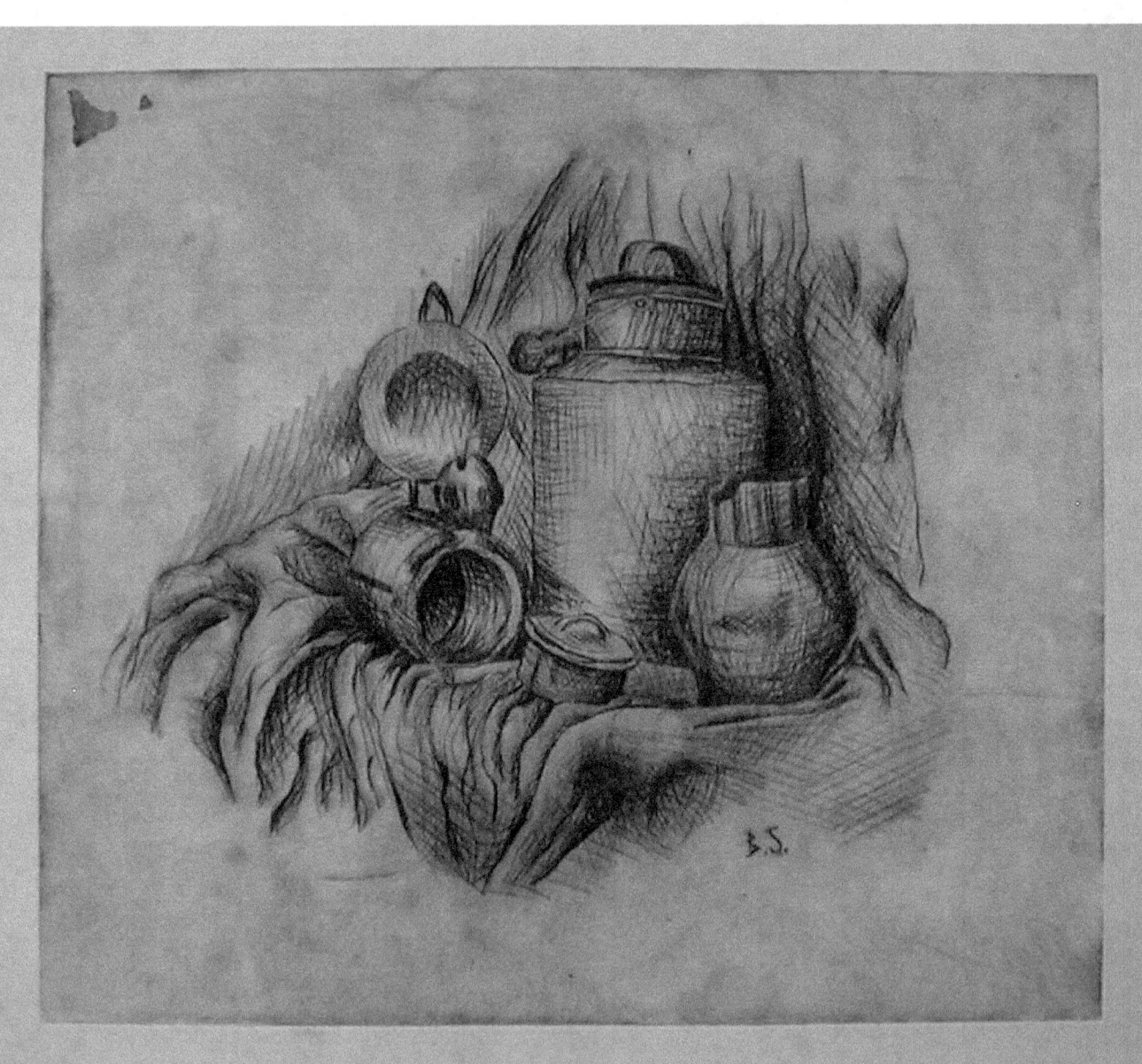

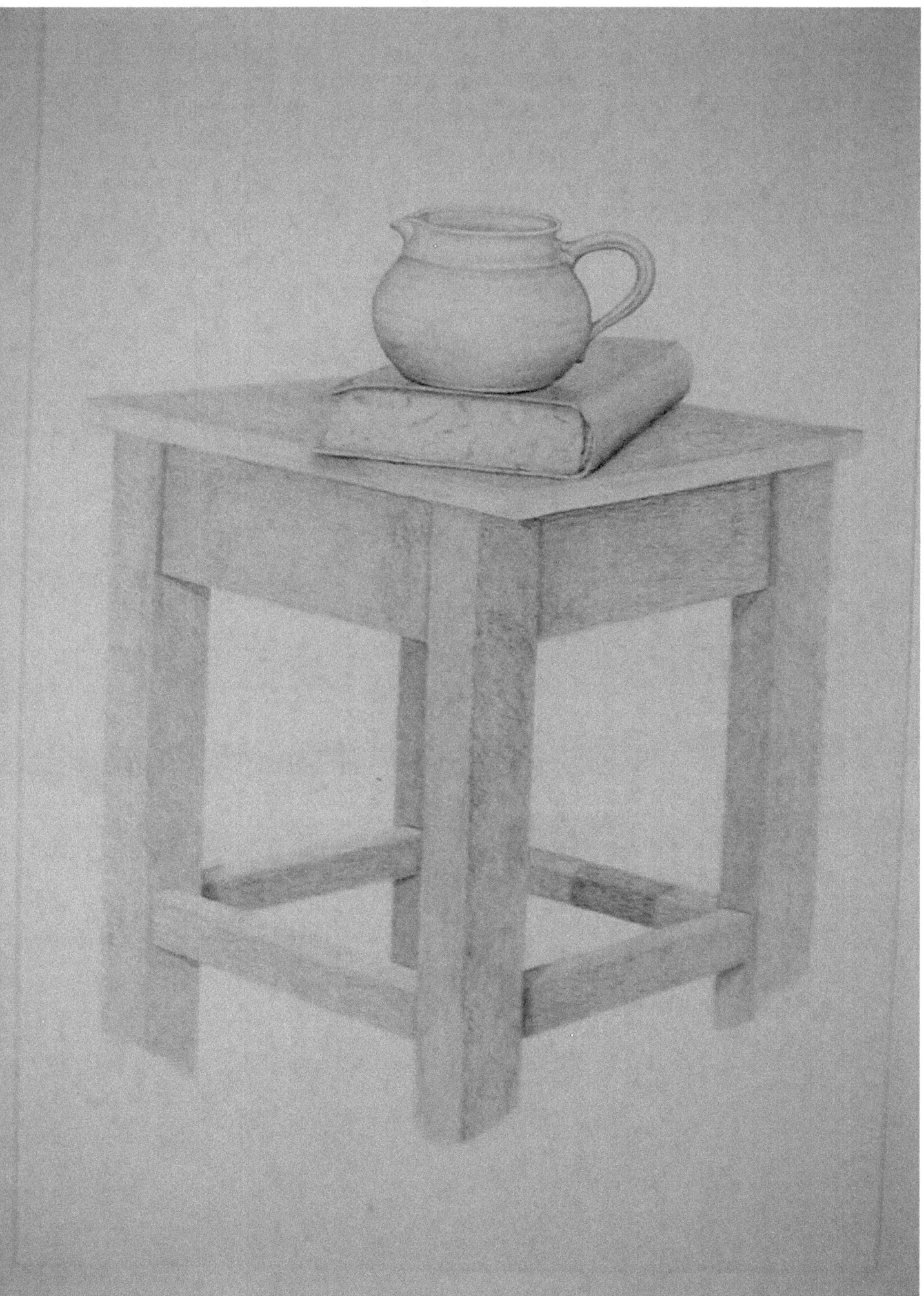

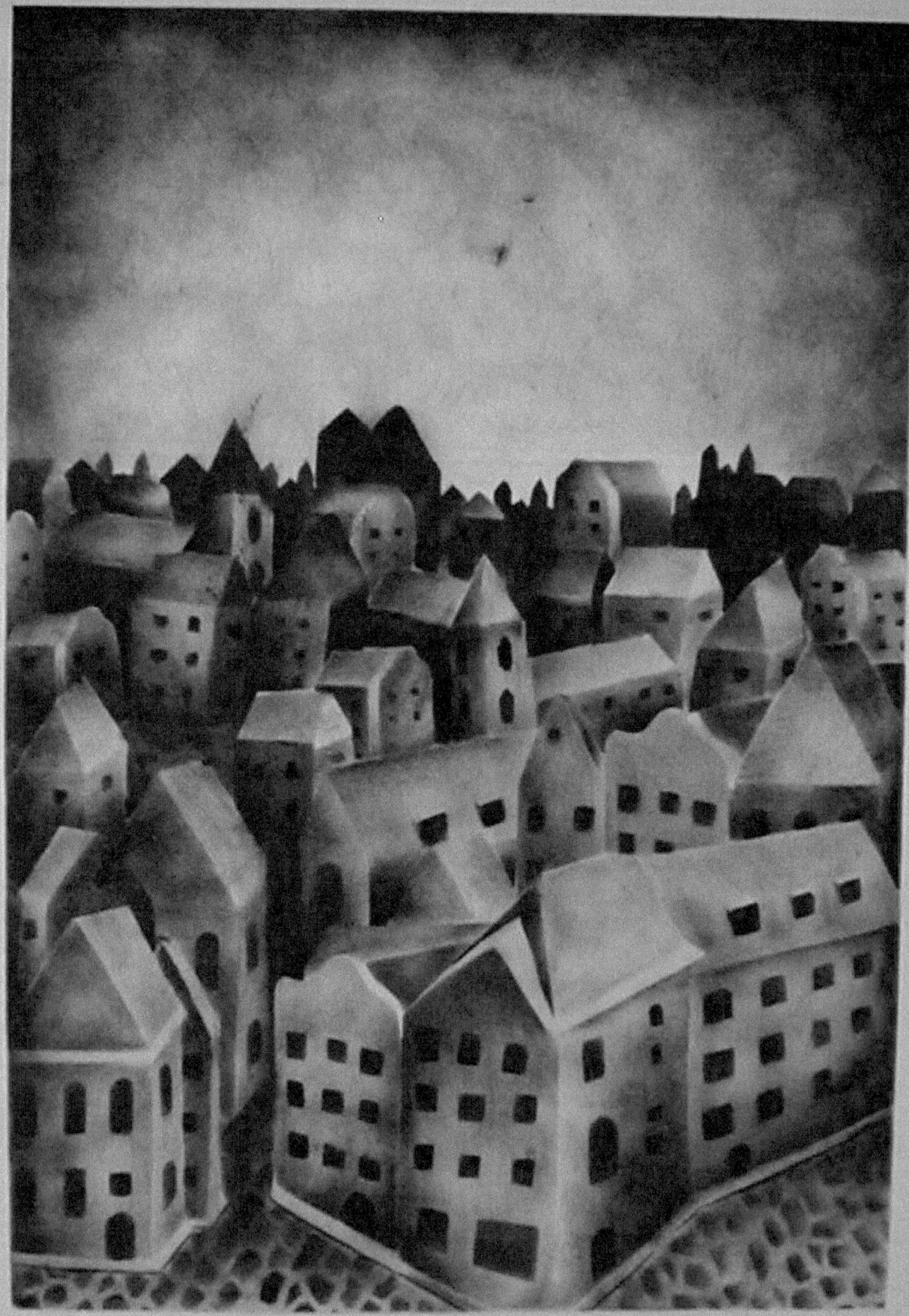

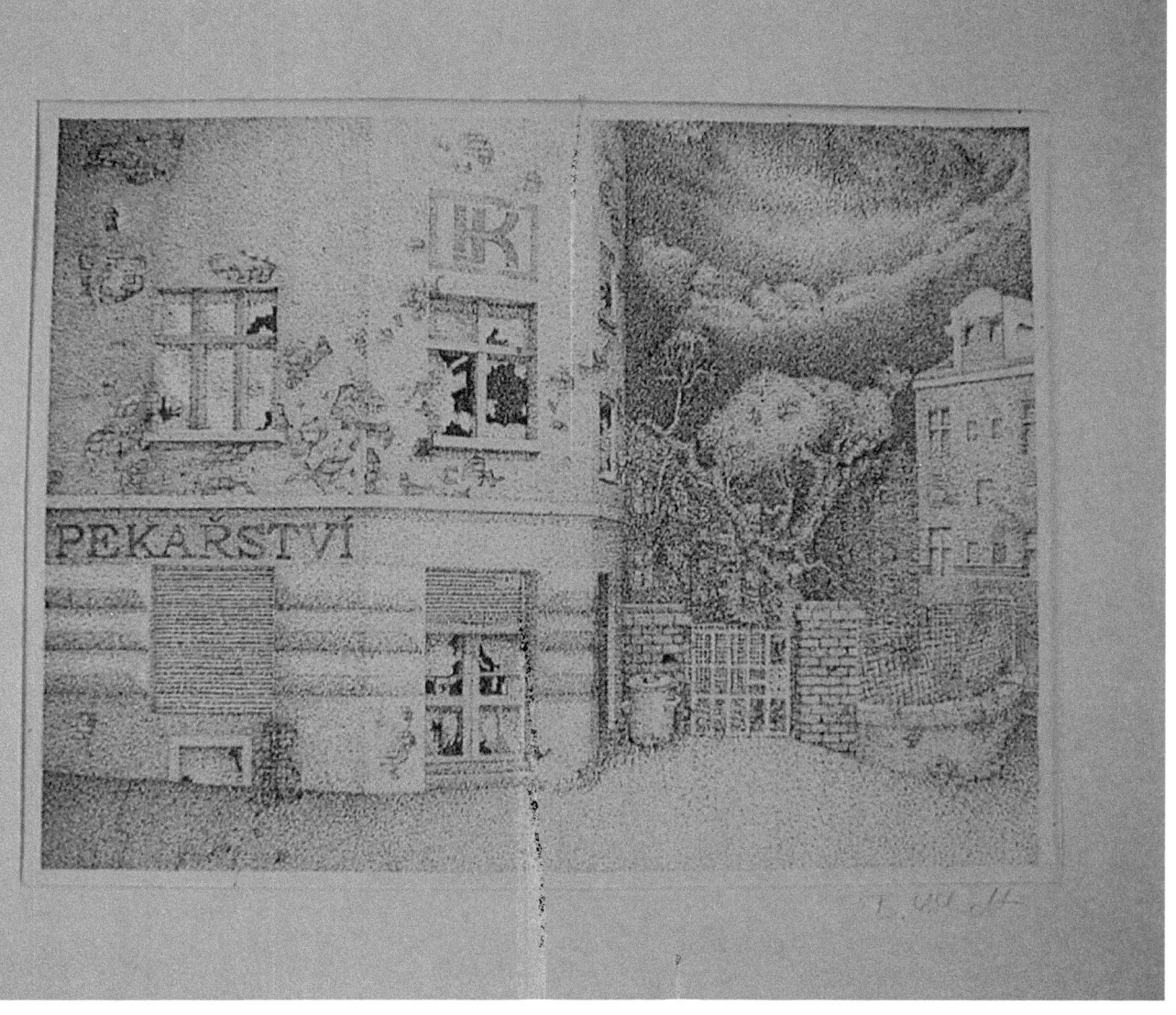

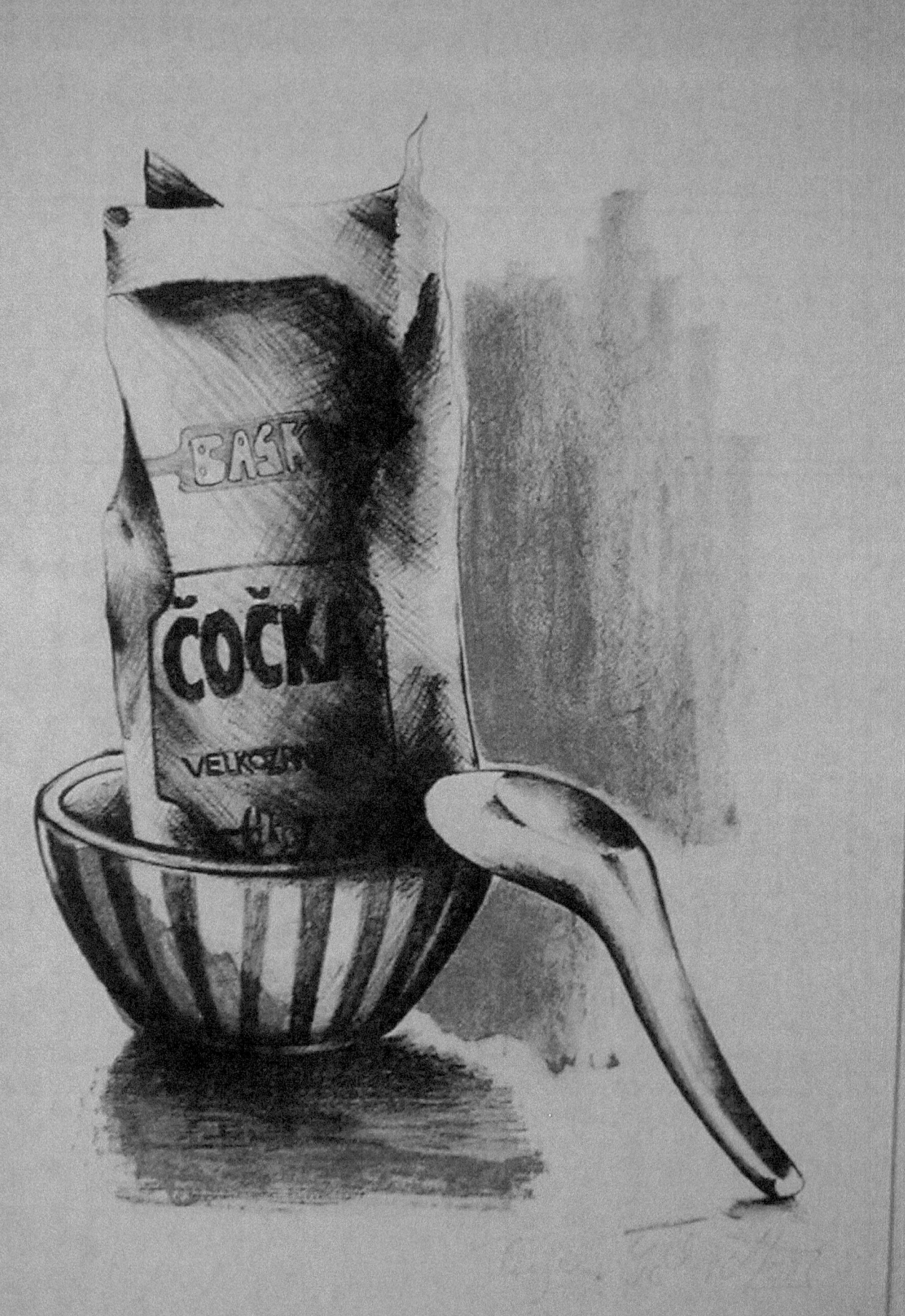

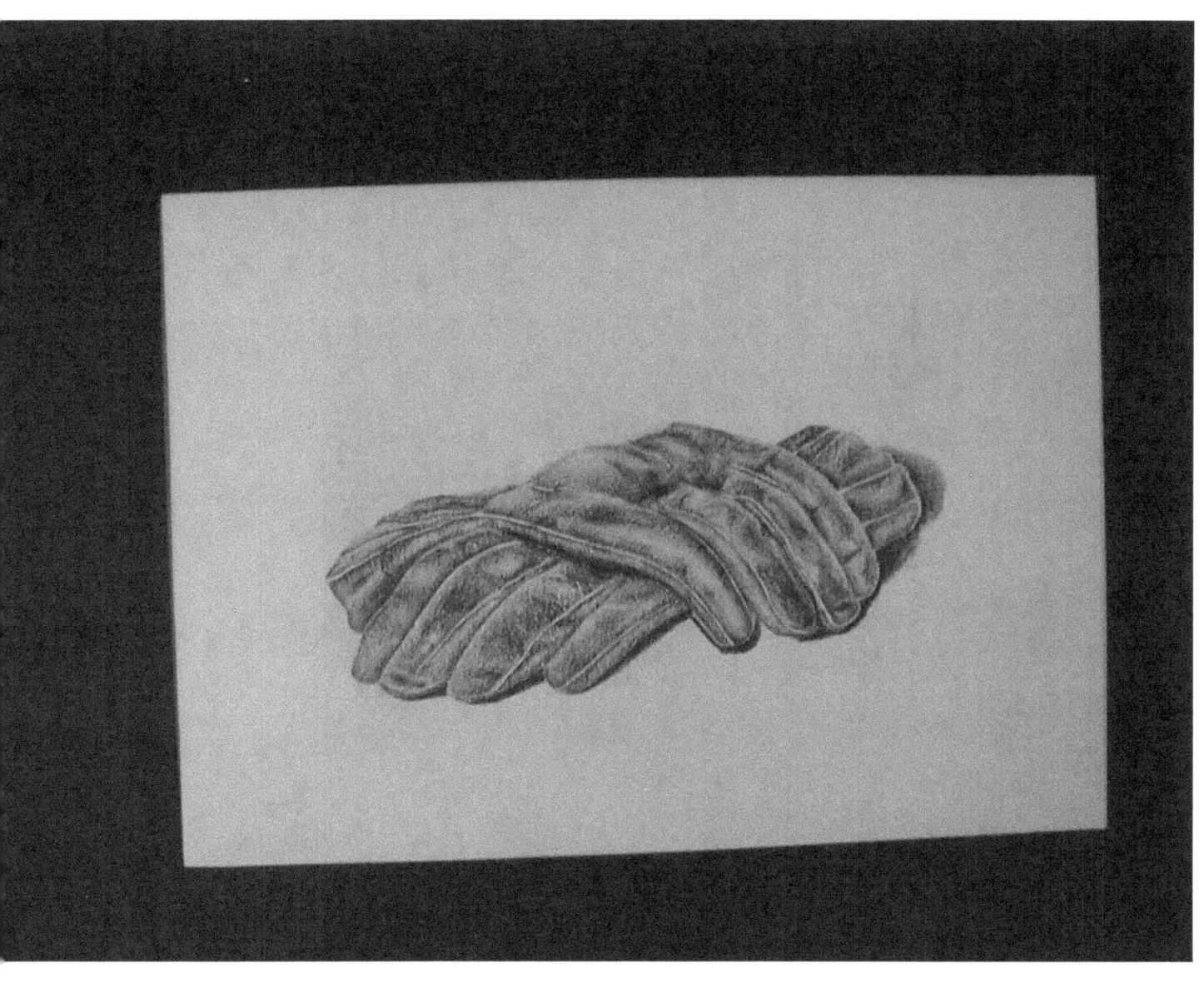

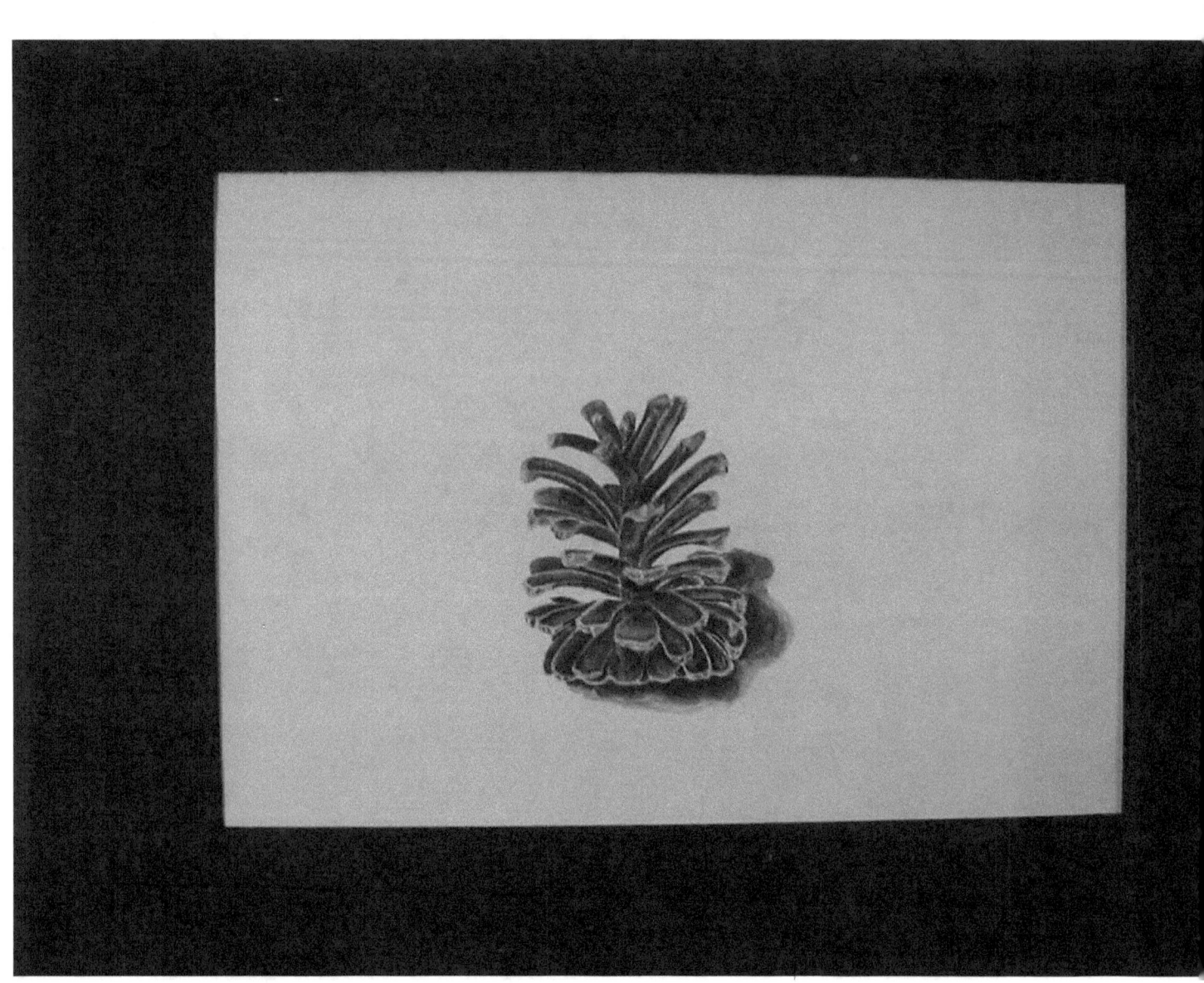

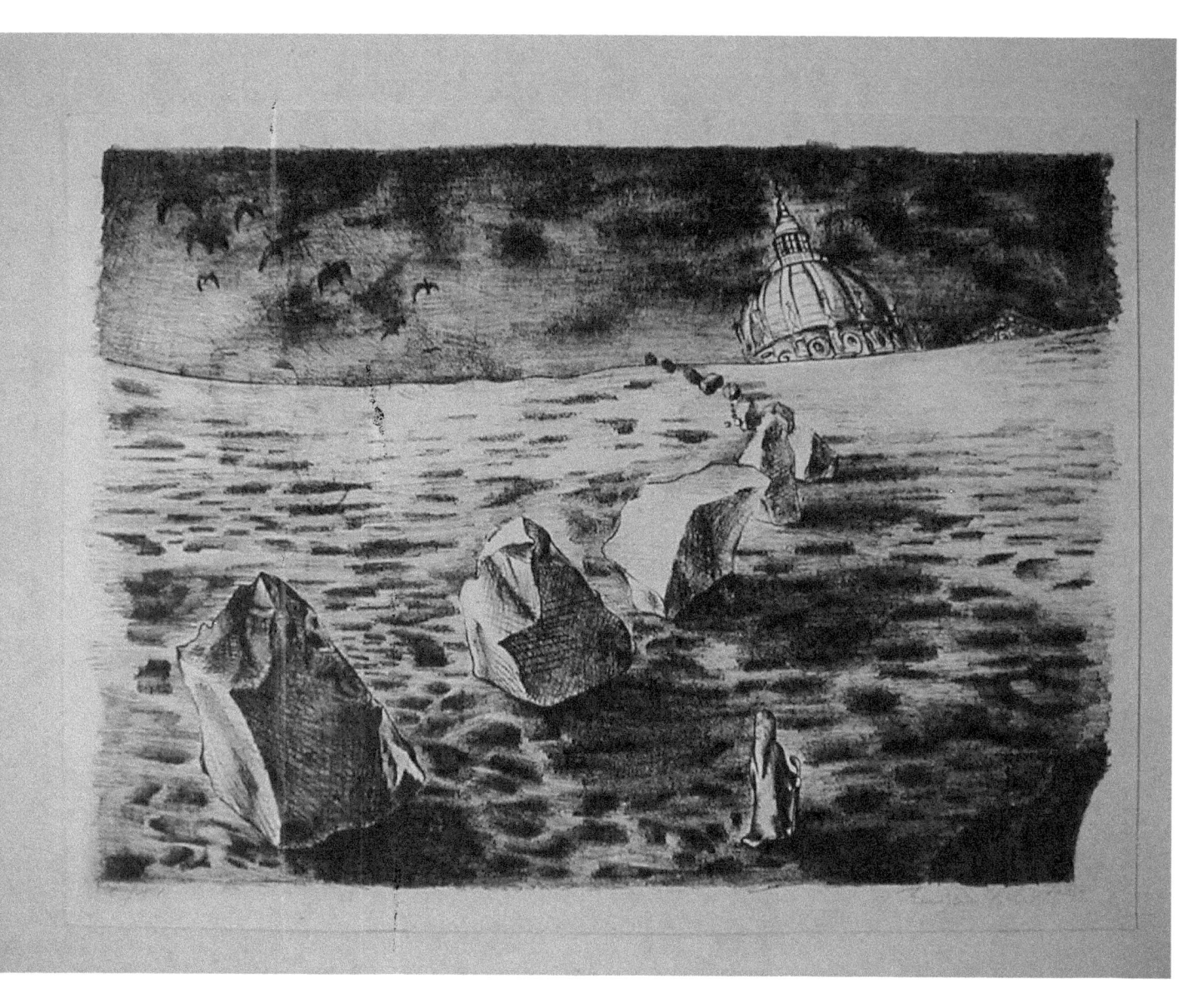

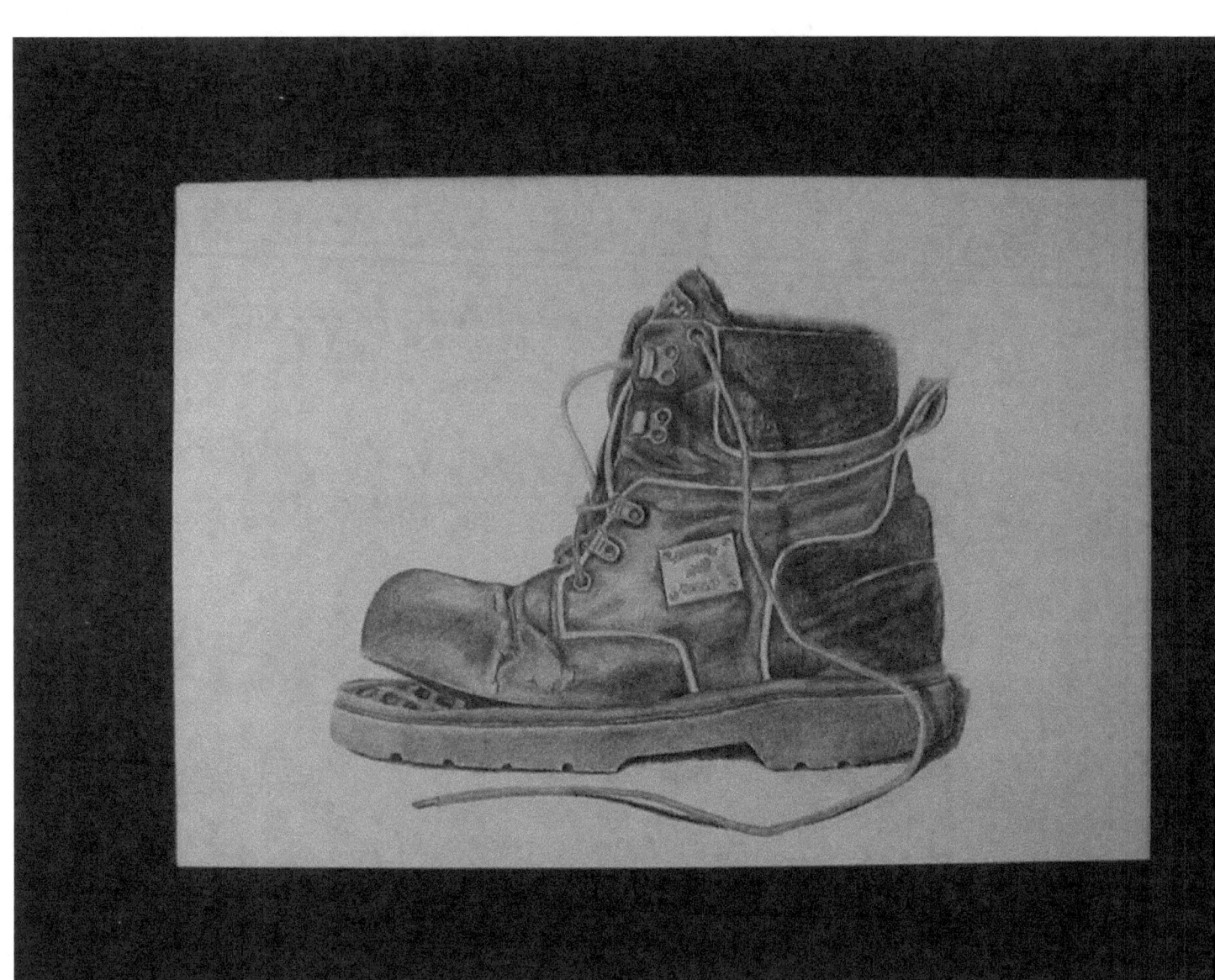

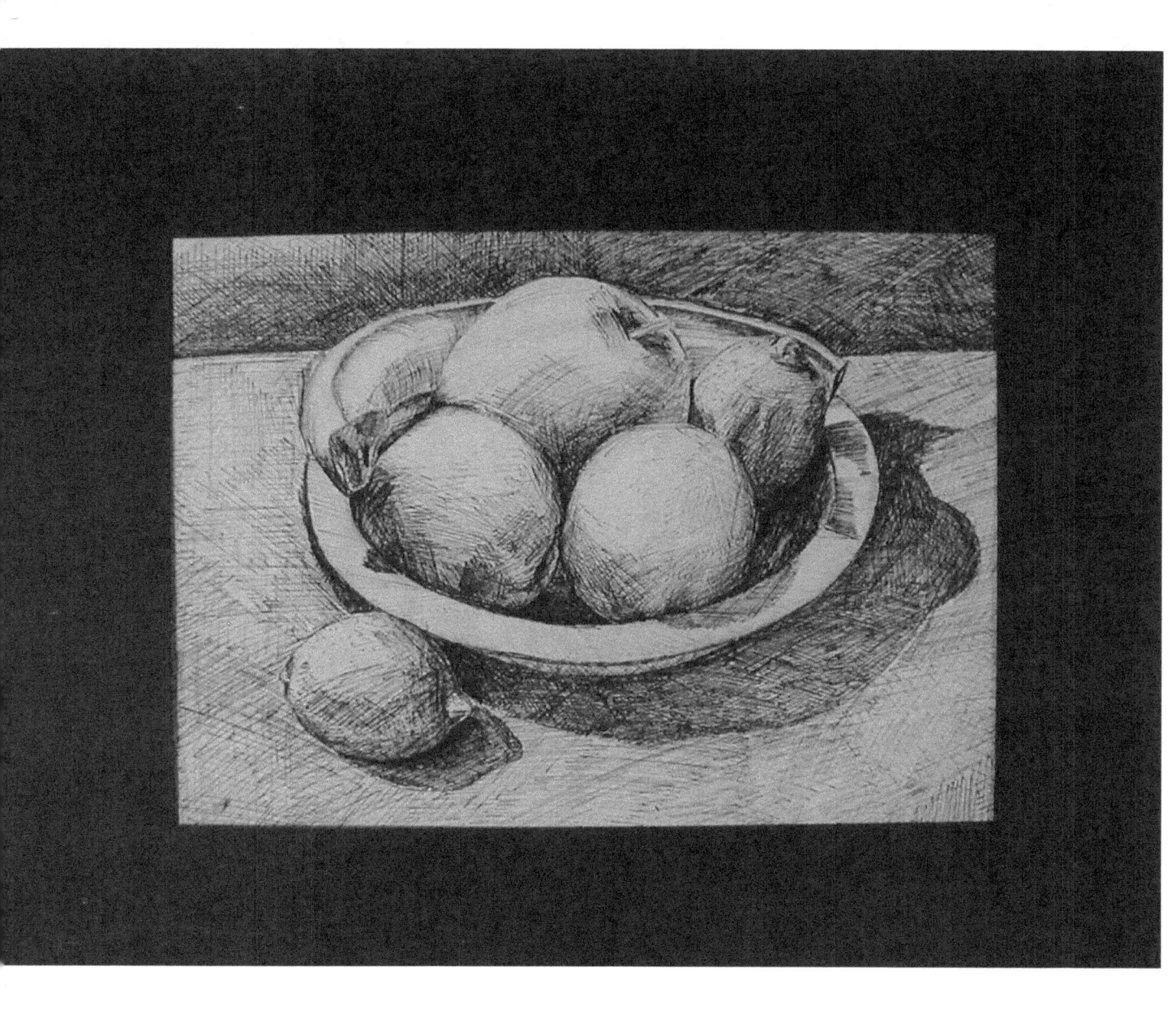

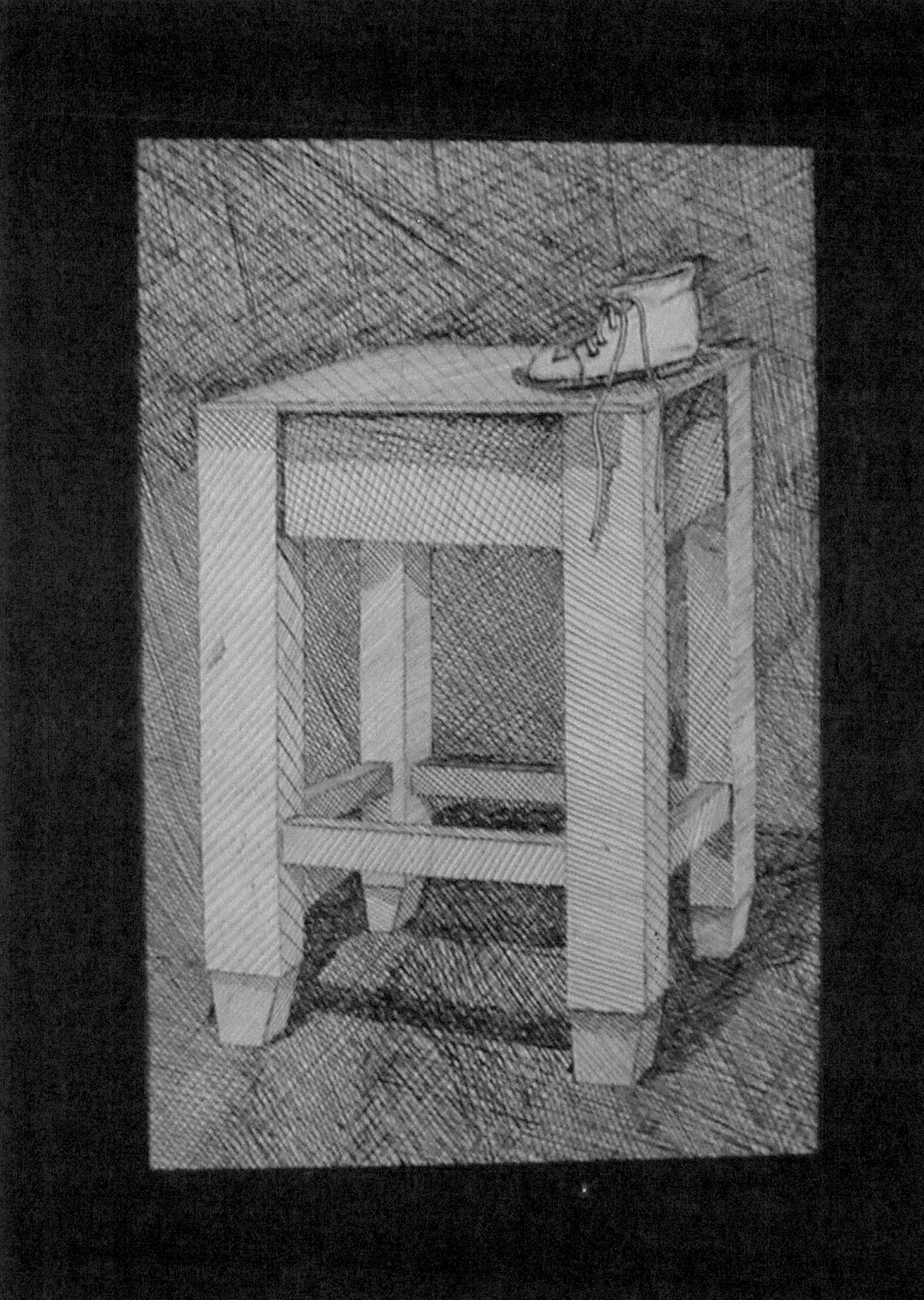

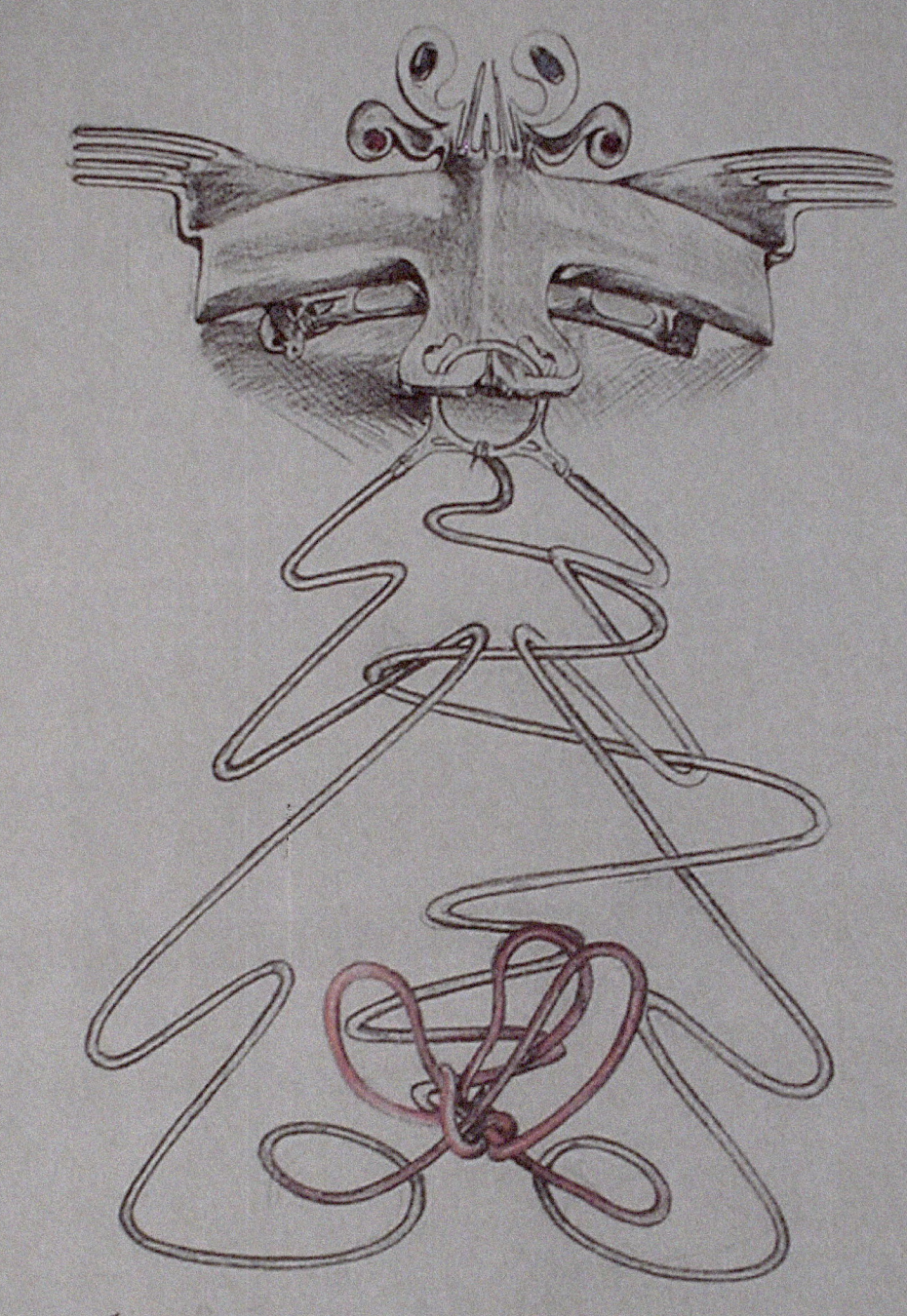

PHOENIX

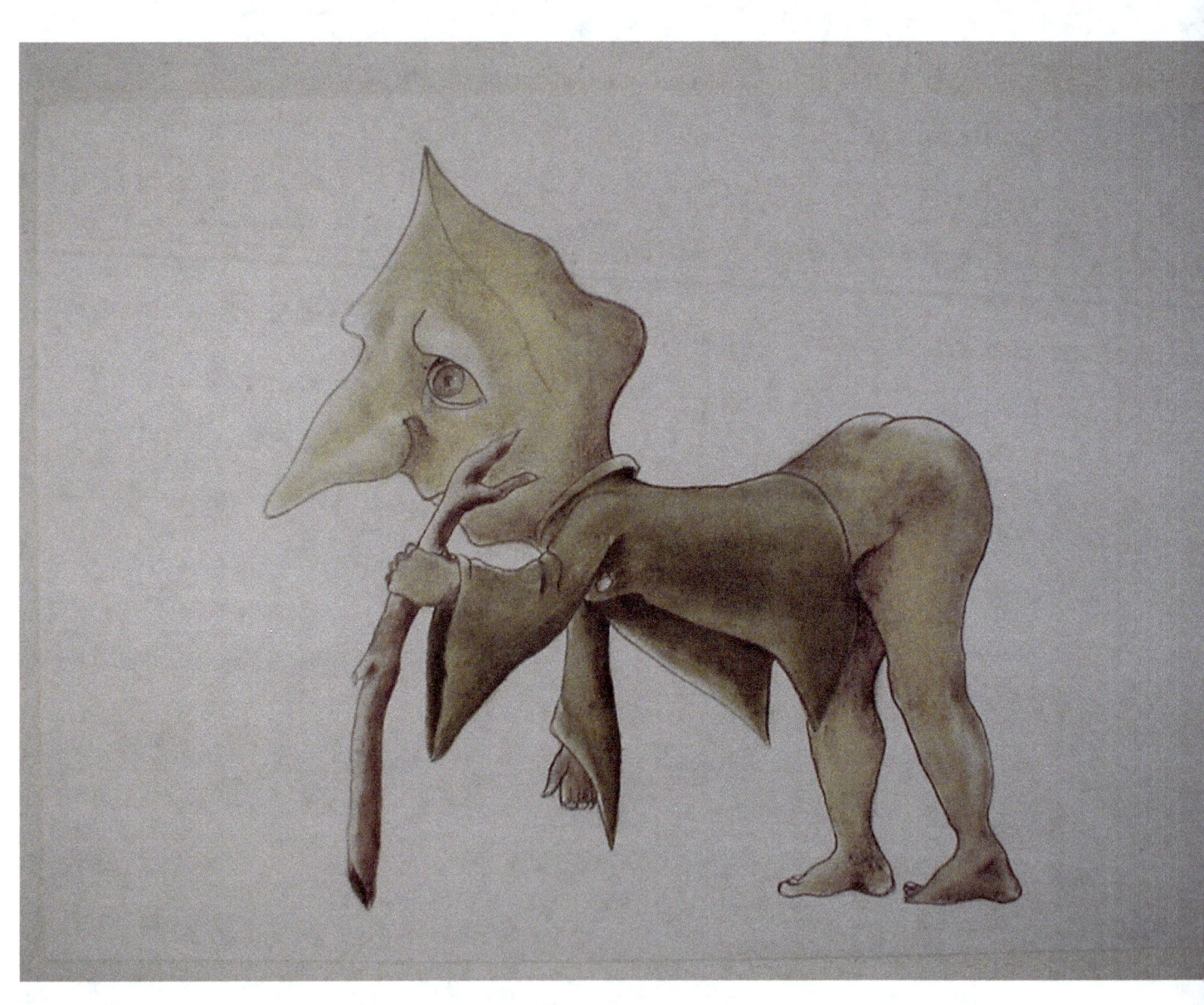

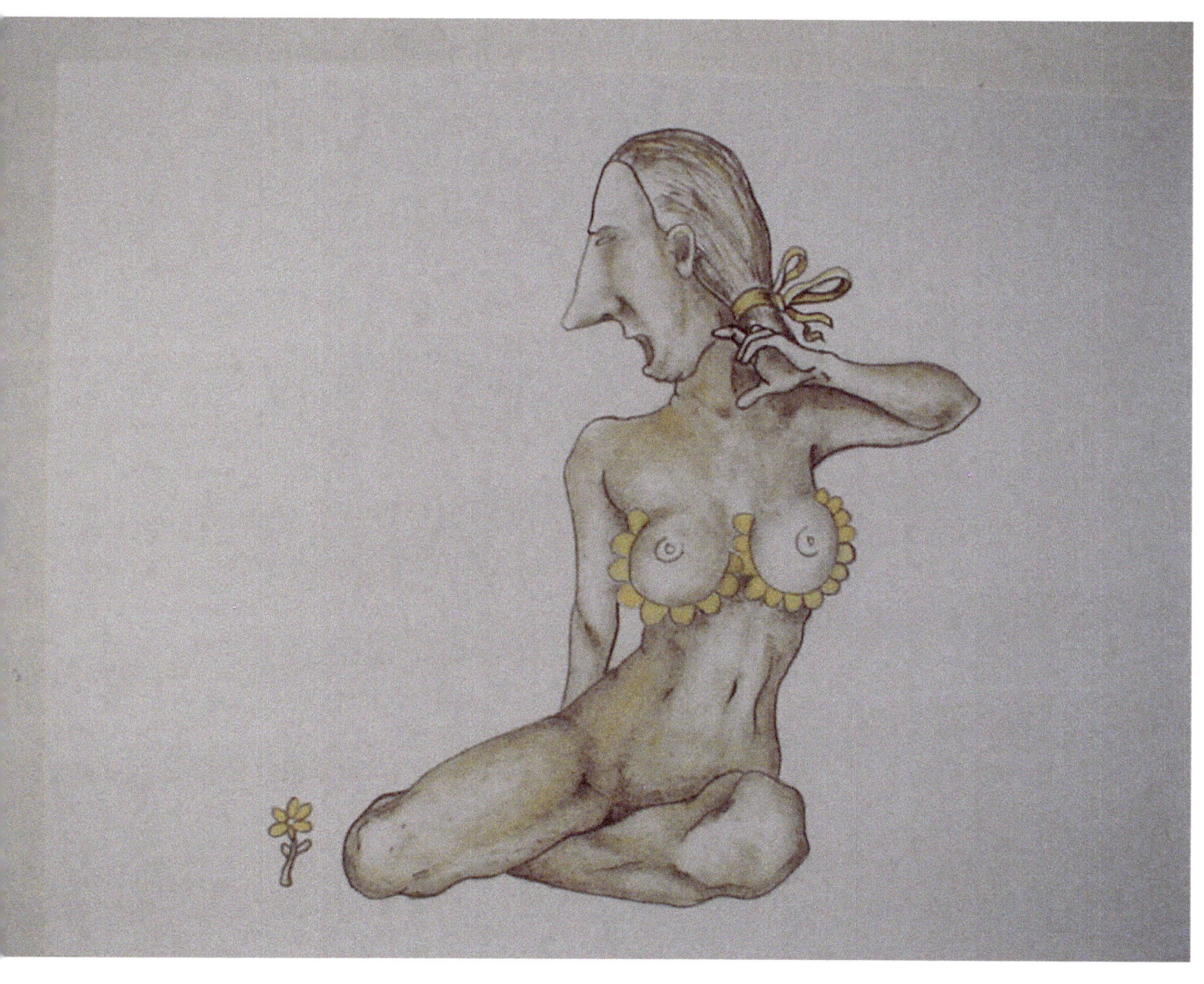

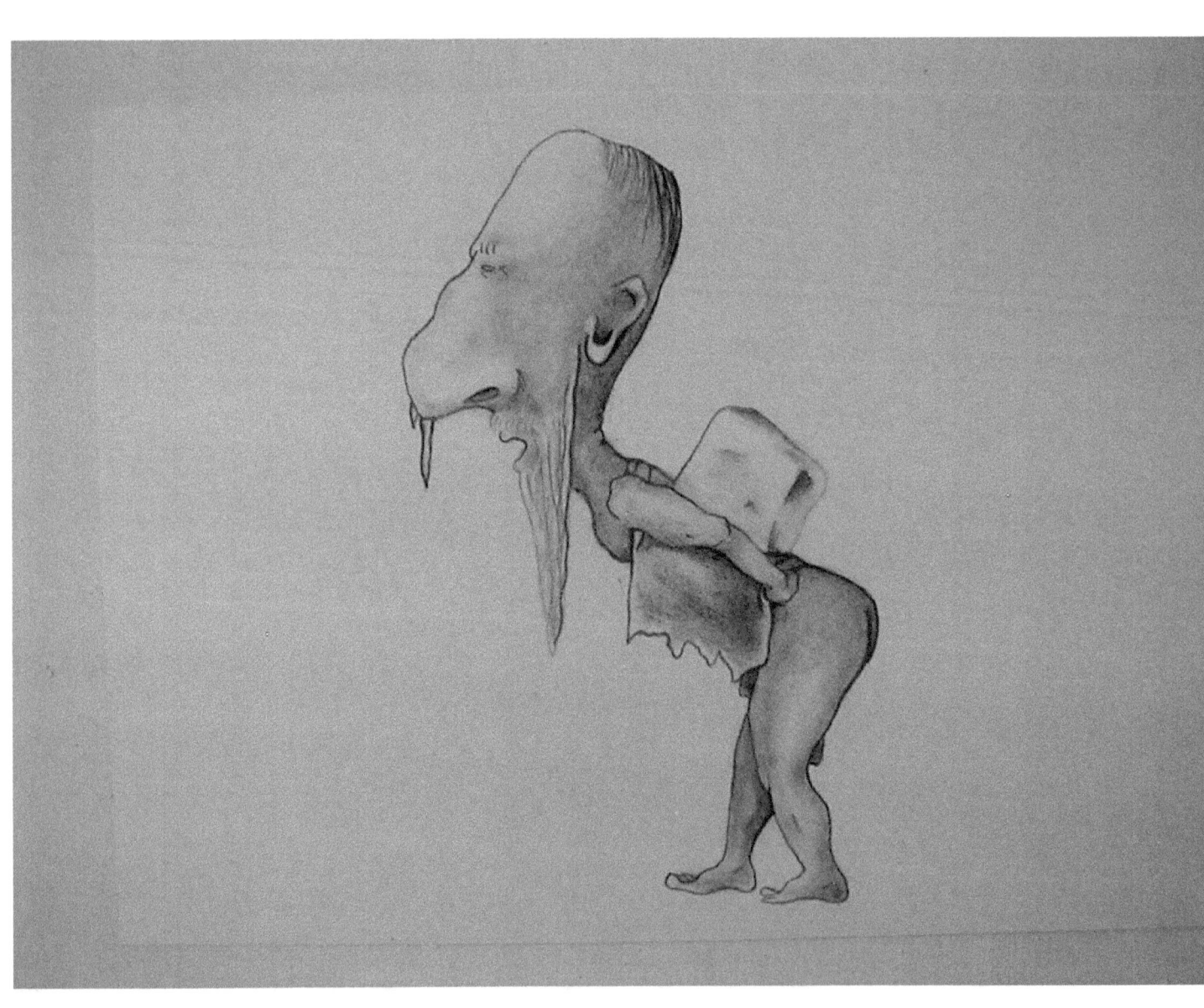

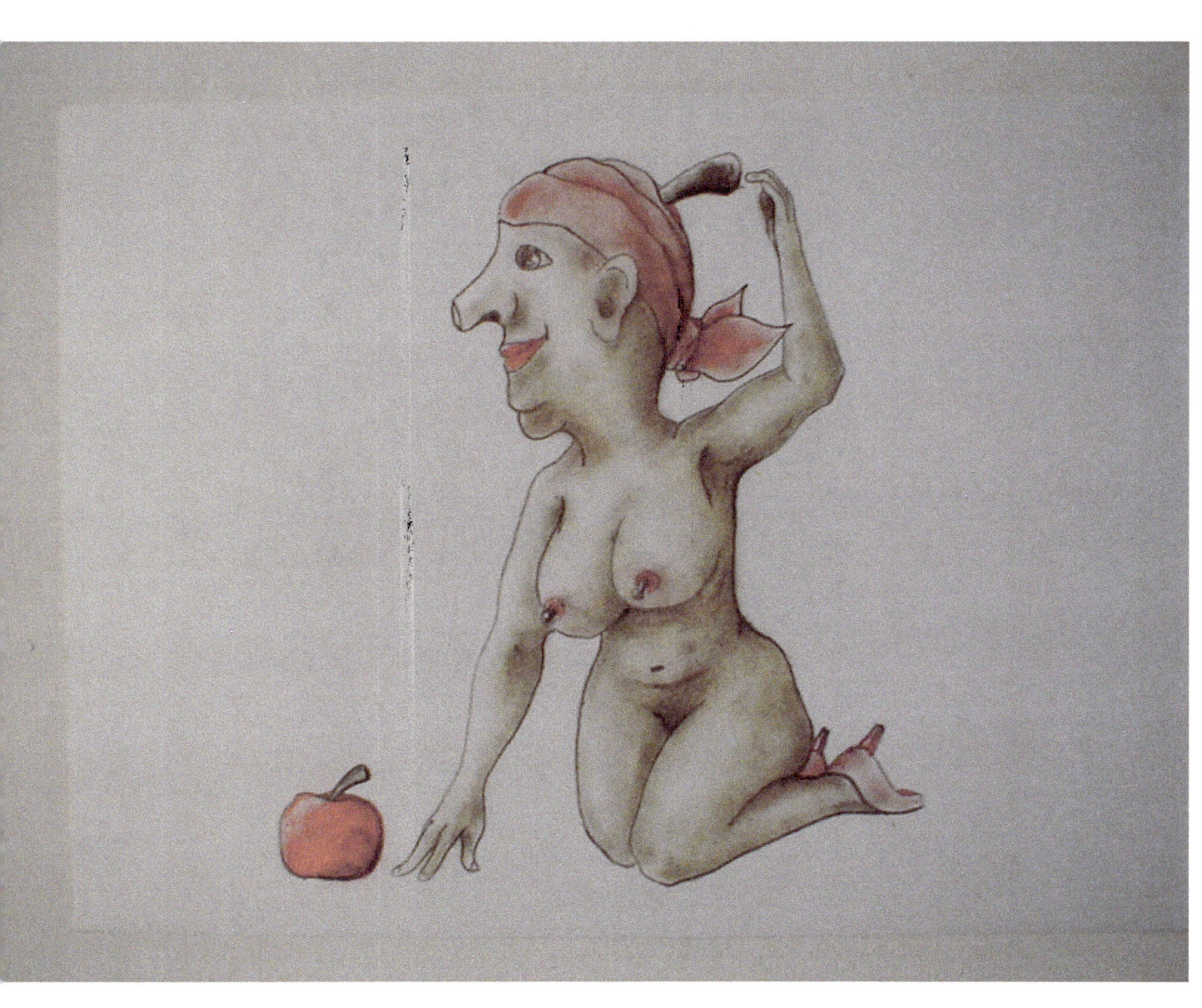

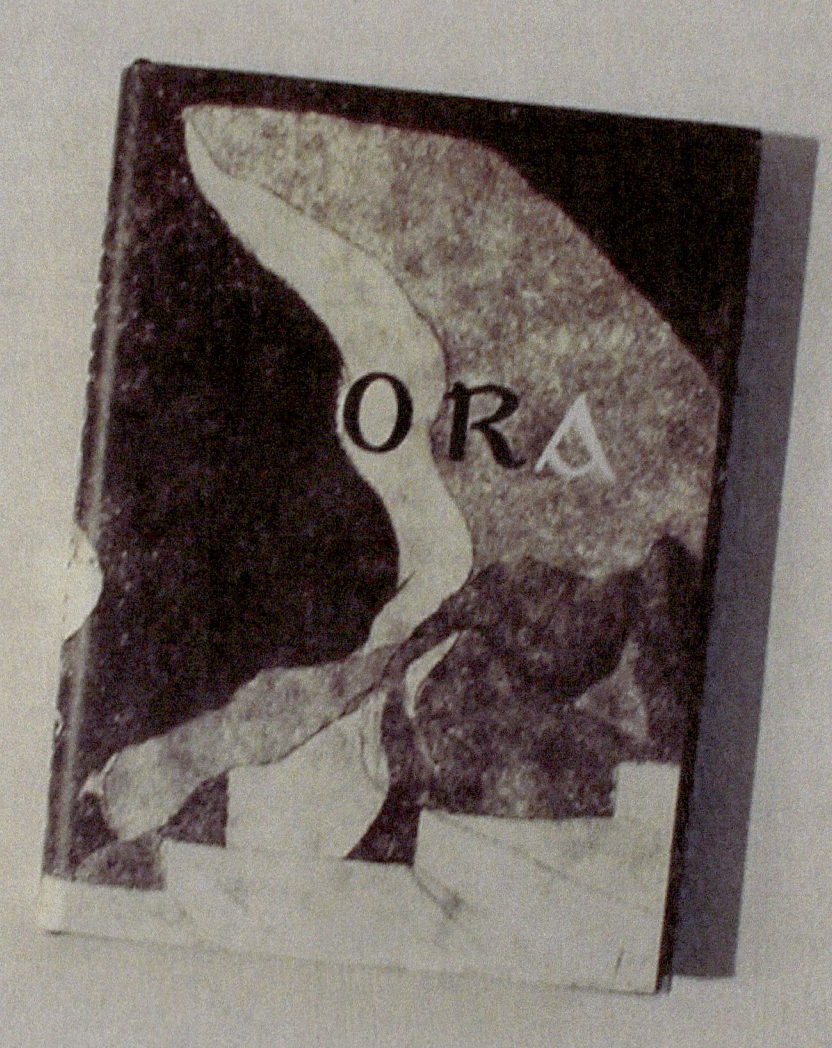

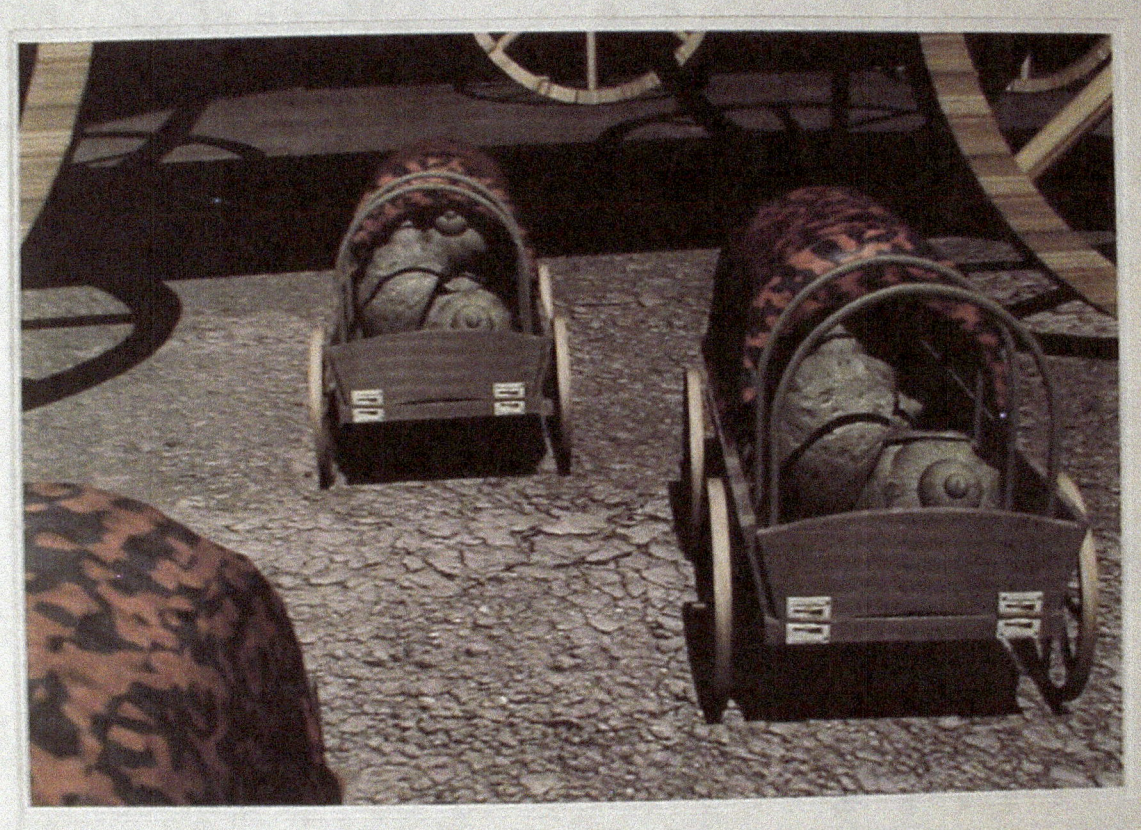

Březen Duben Květen

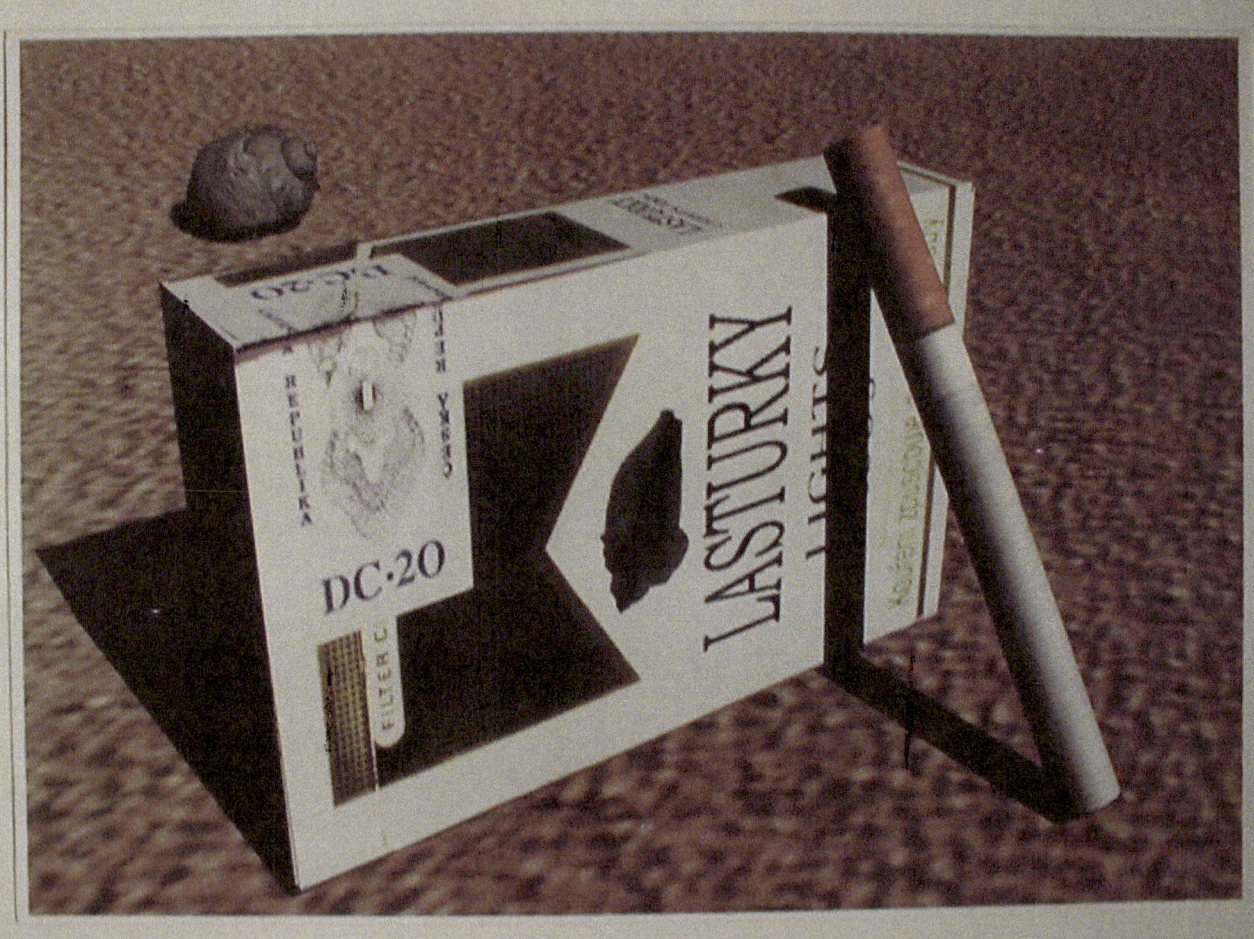

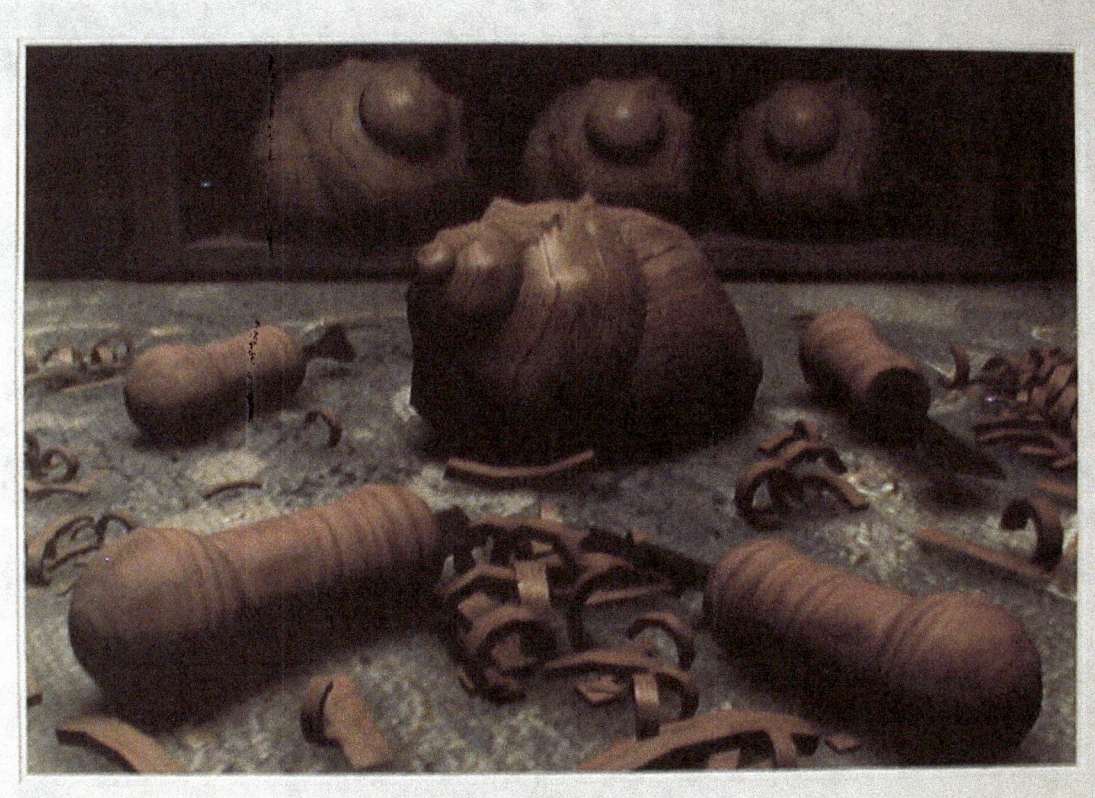

Září   Říjen   Listopad

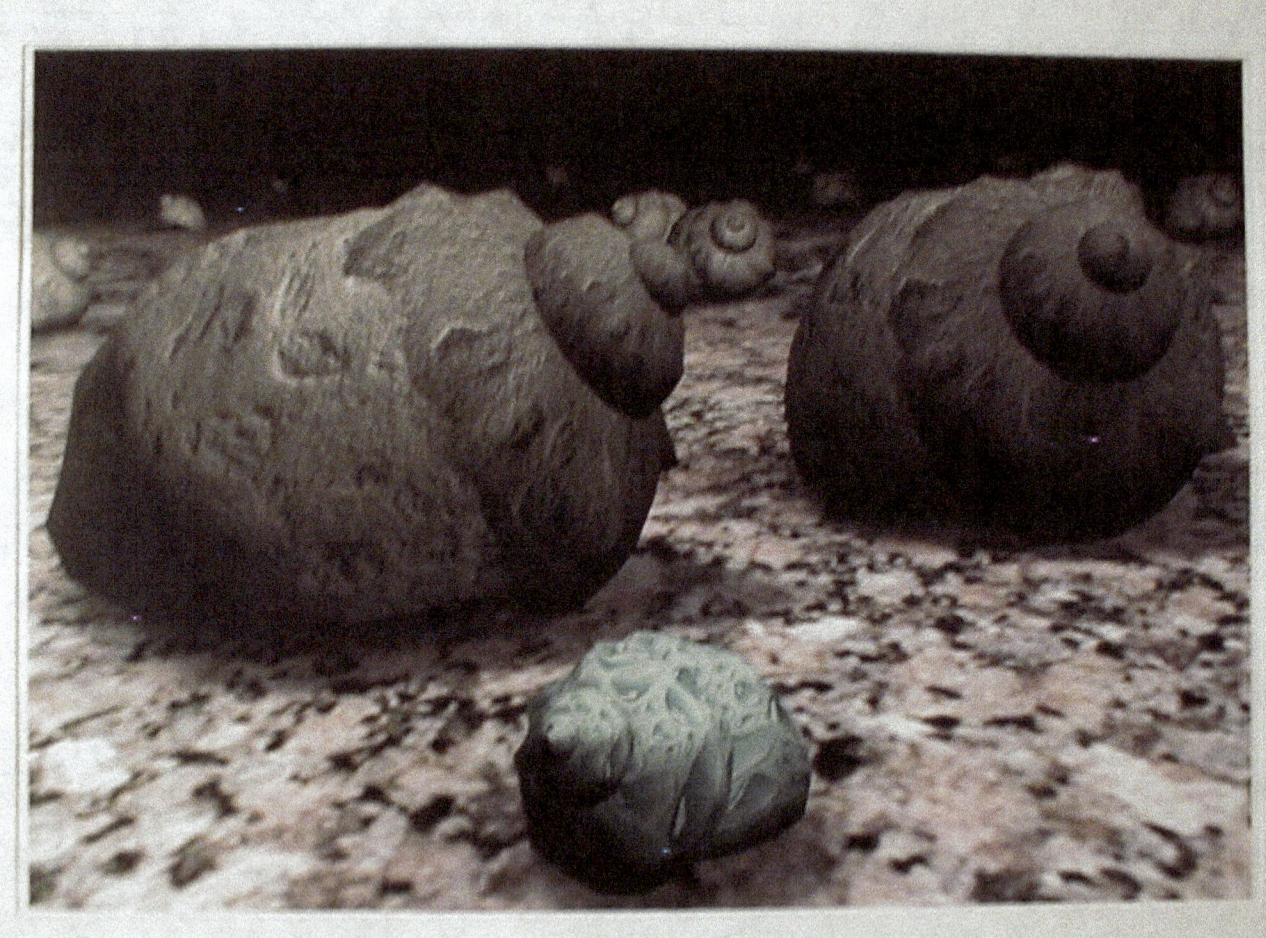

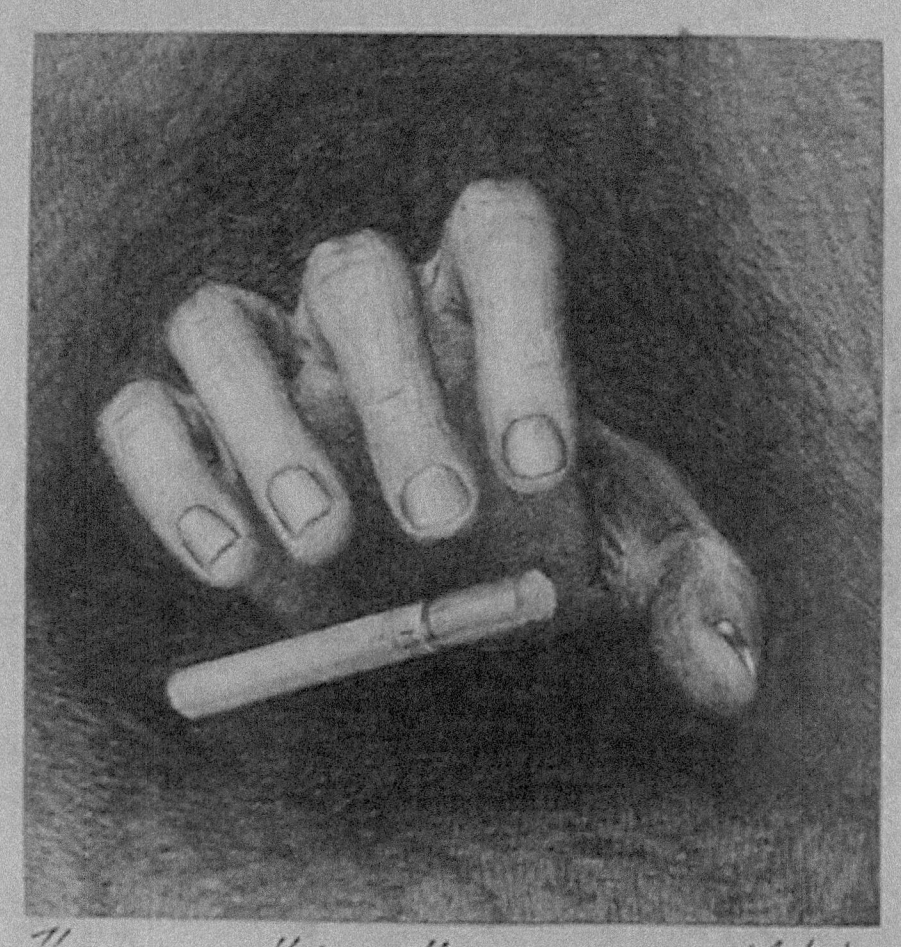

1/1   "vice"   Benjamin Schatt
'06

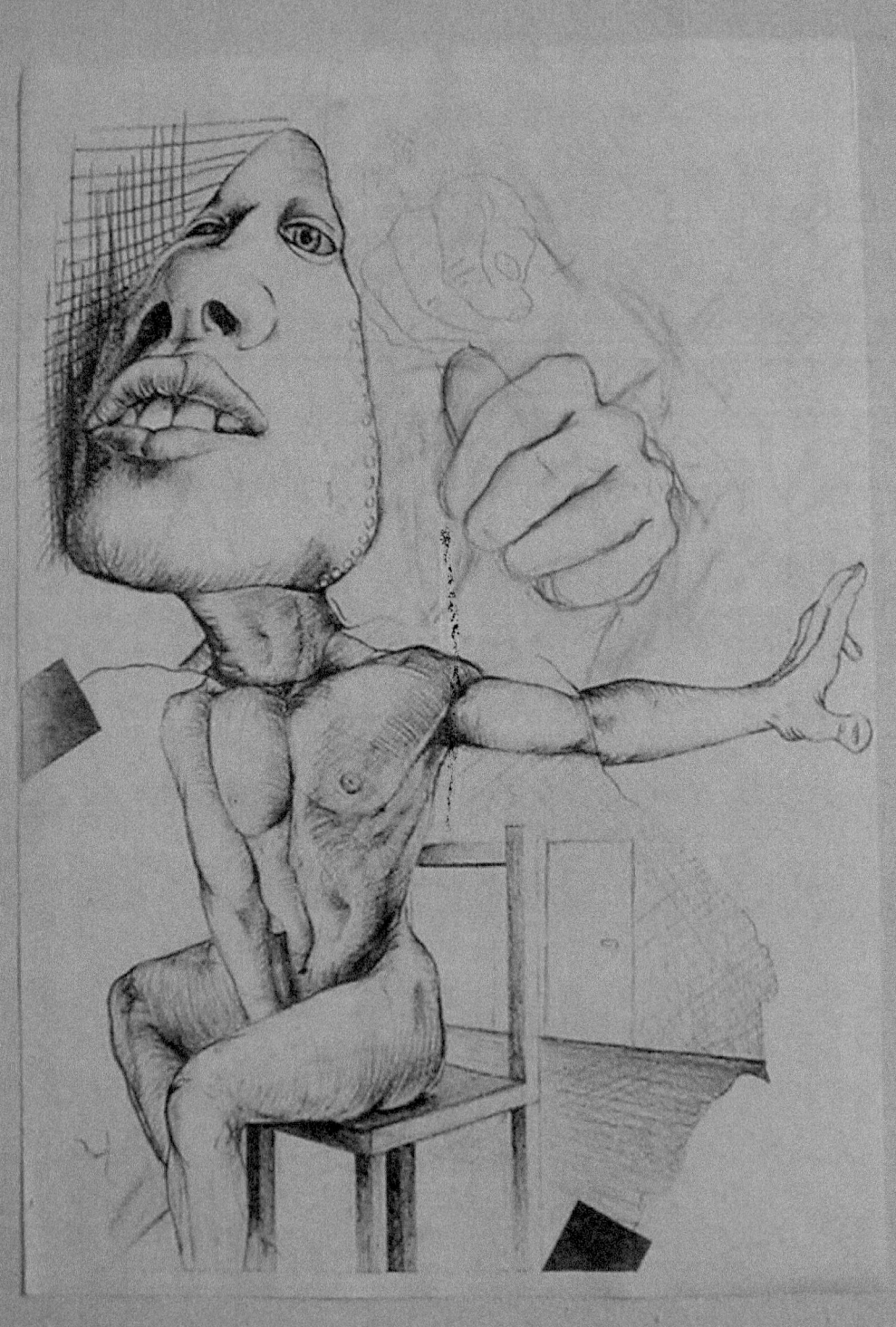

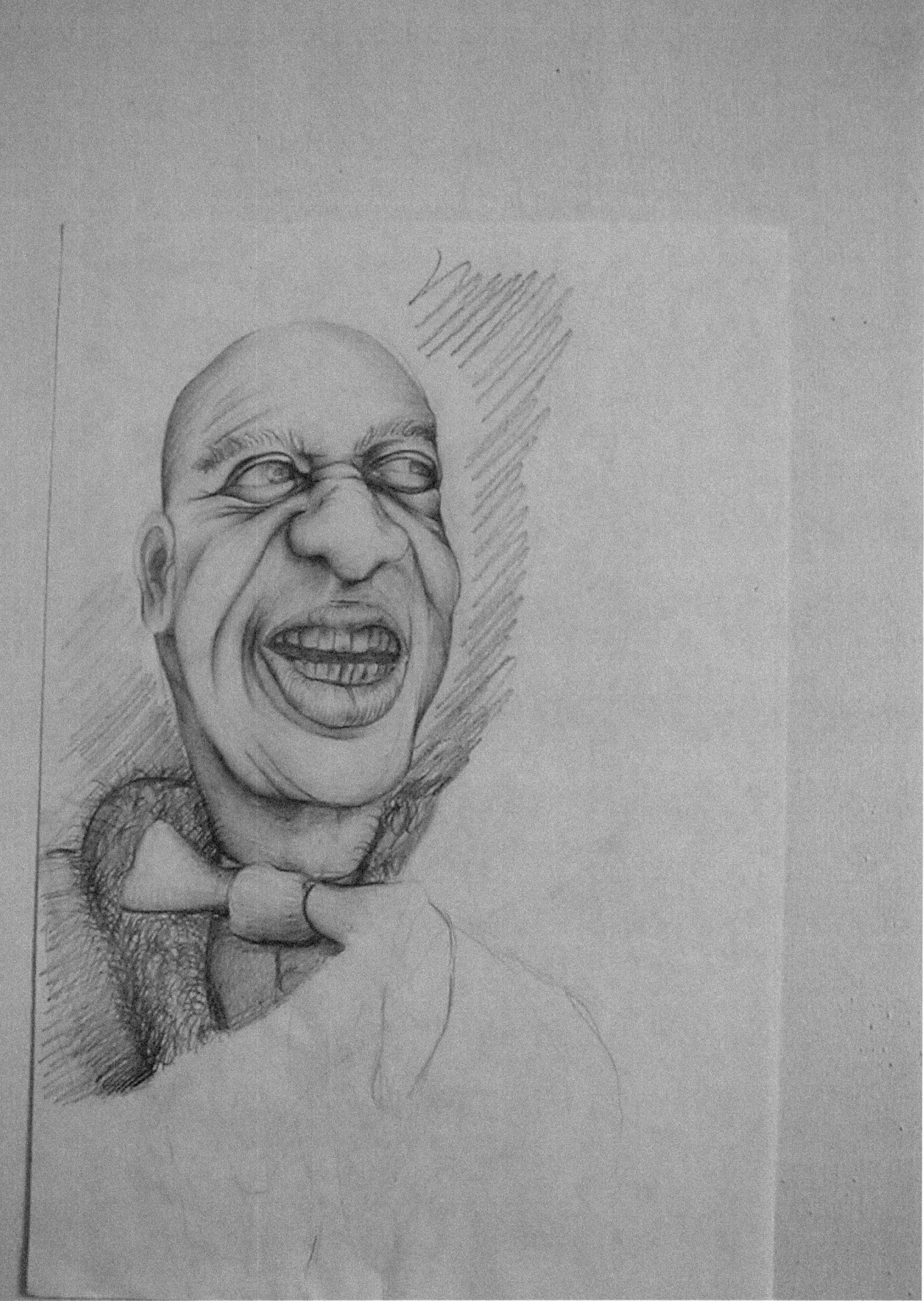

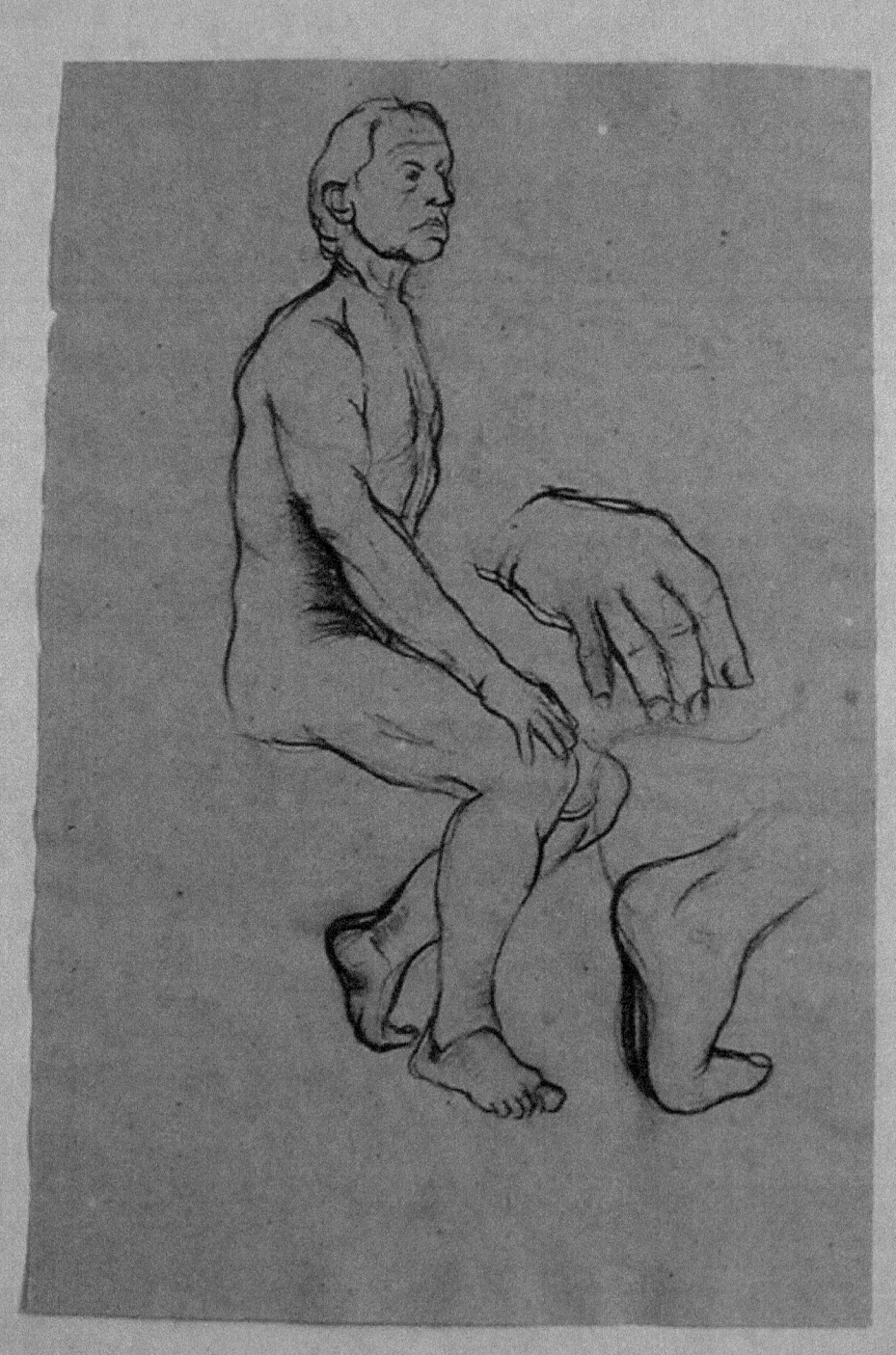

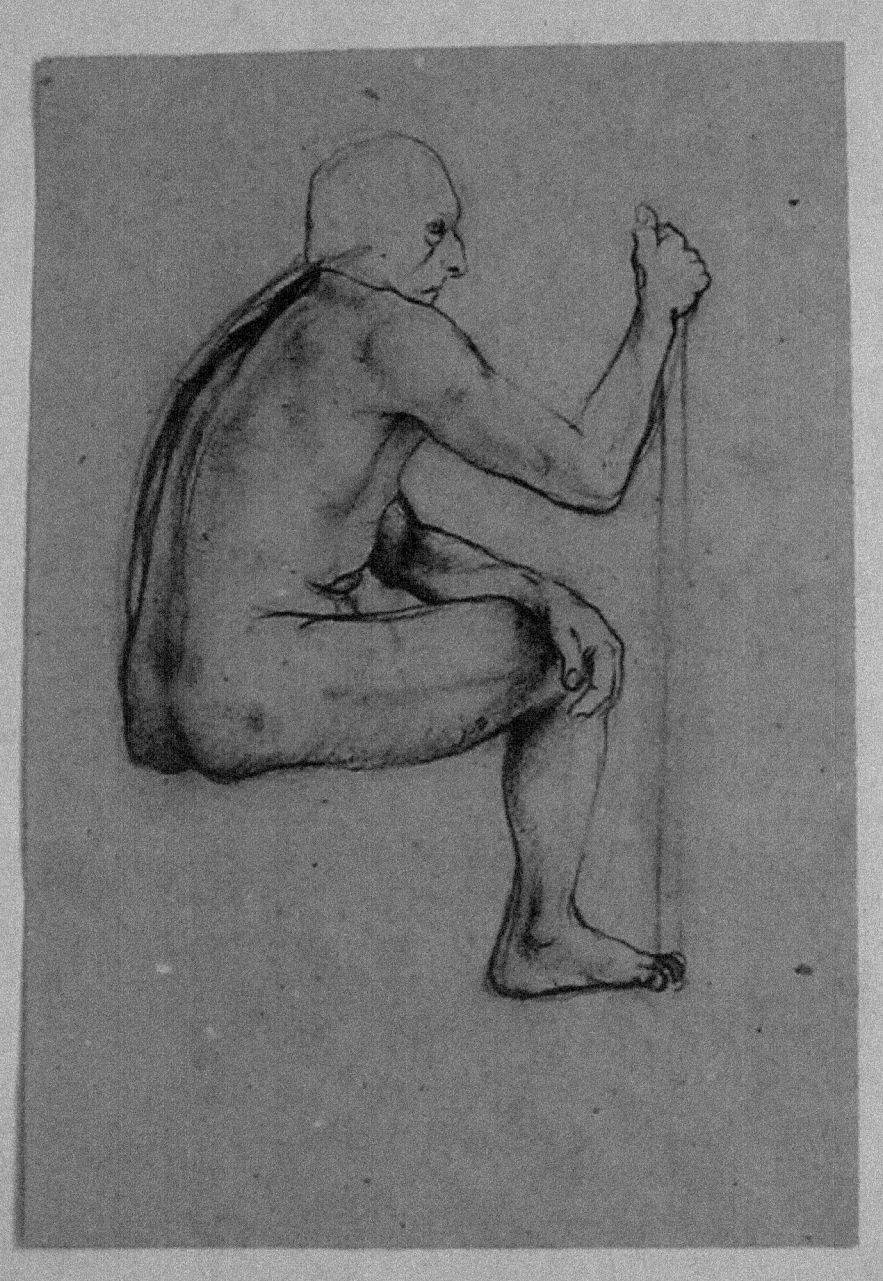

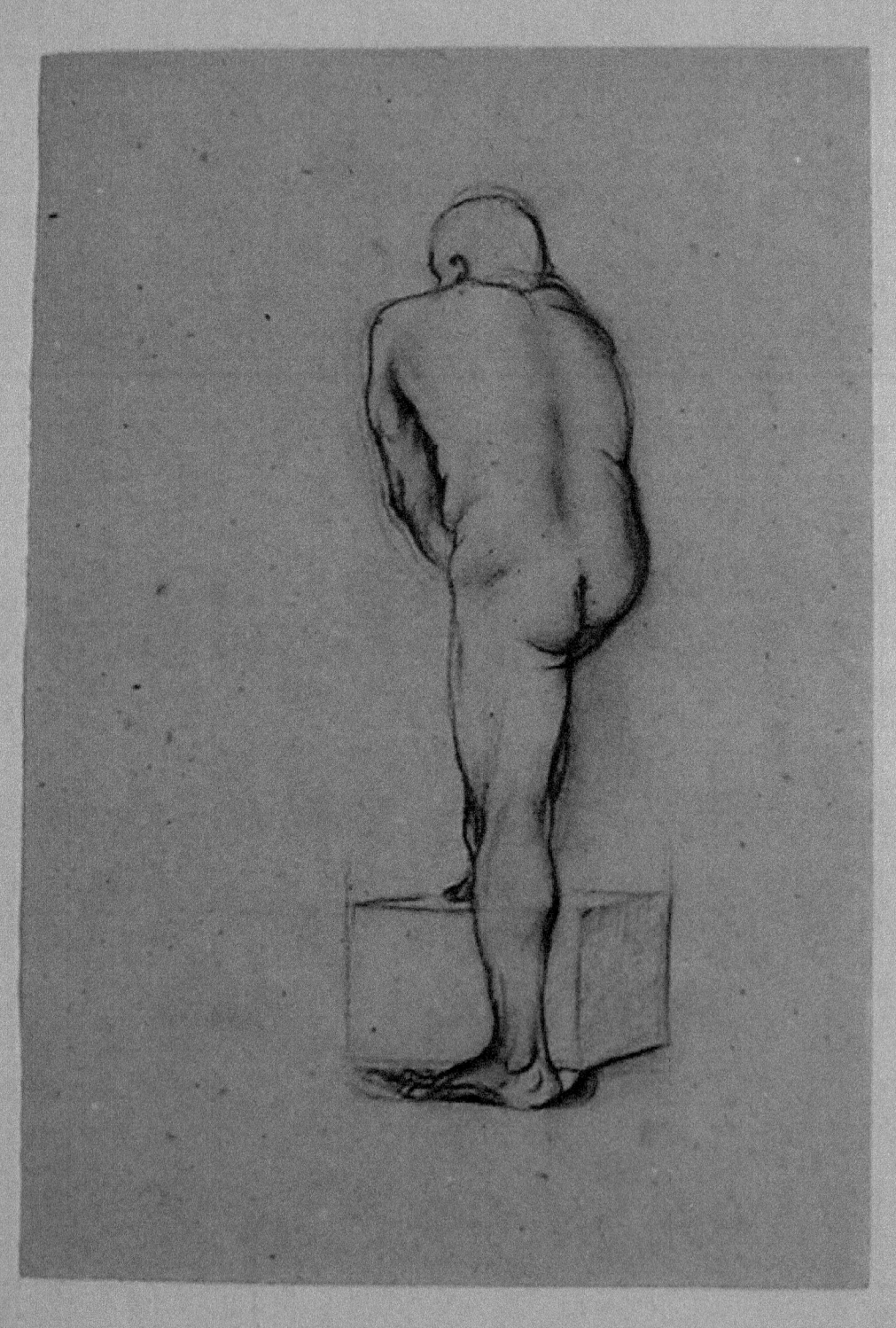

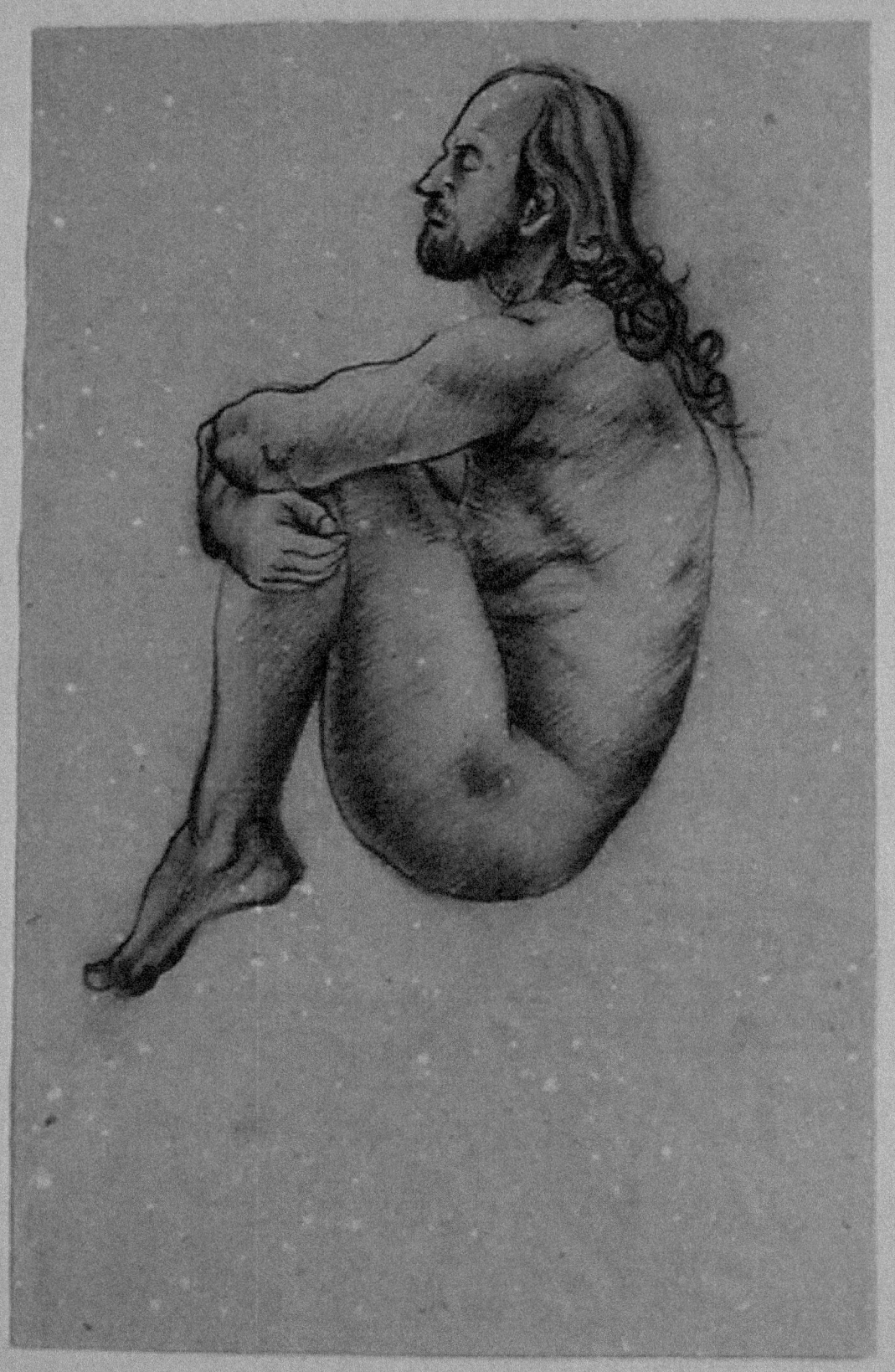

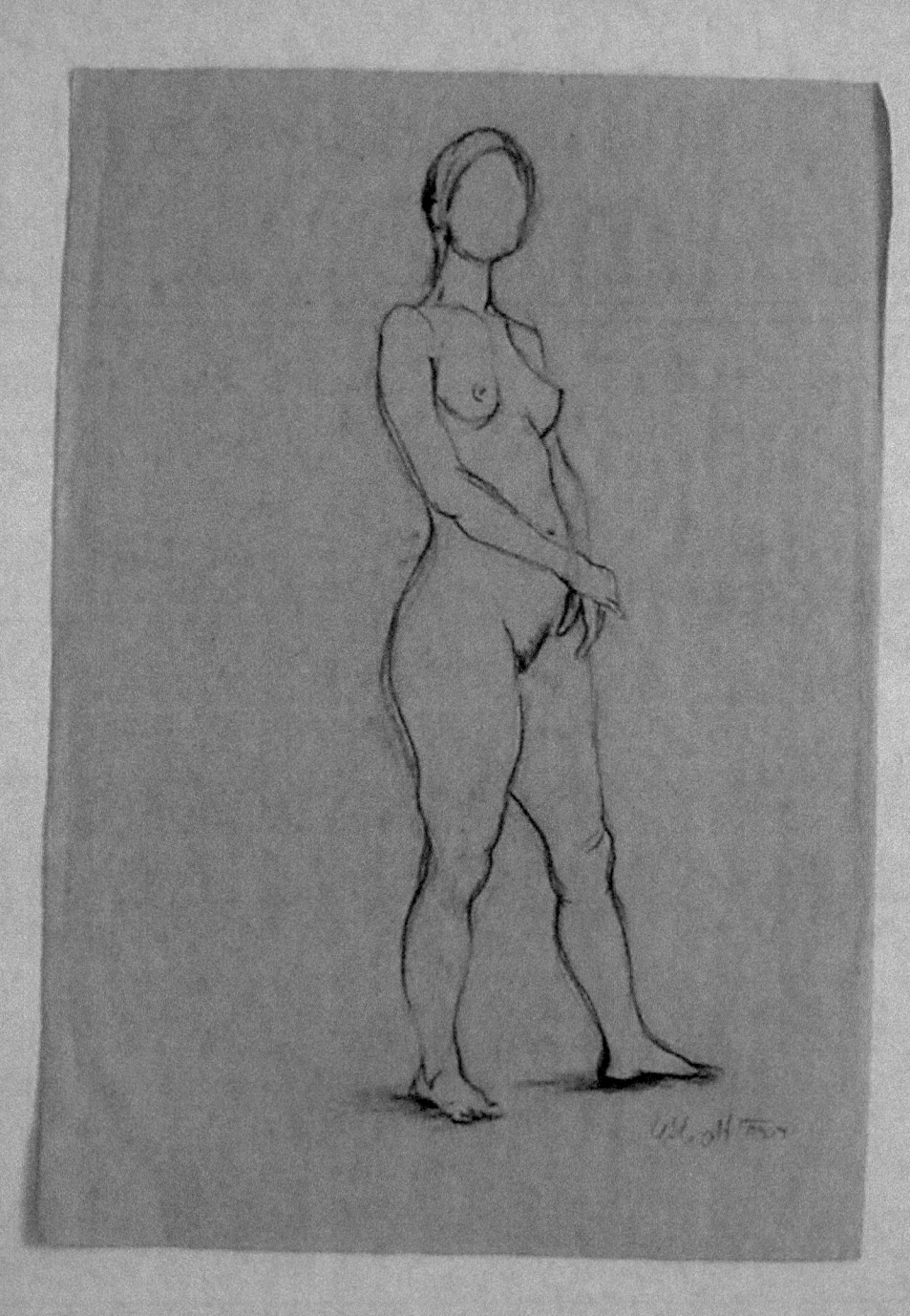

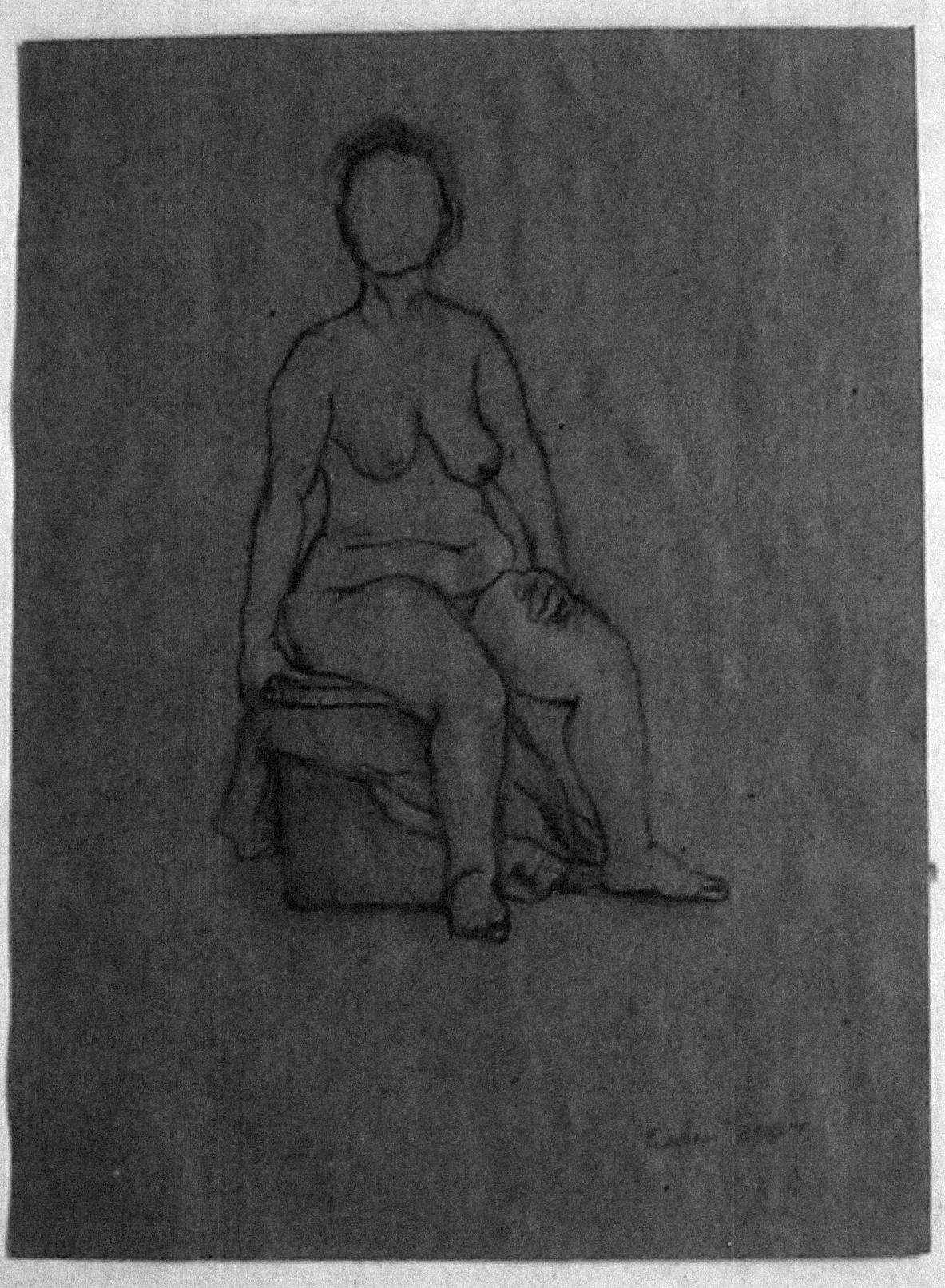

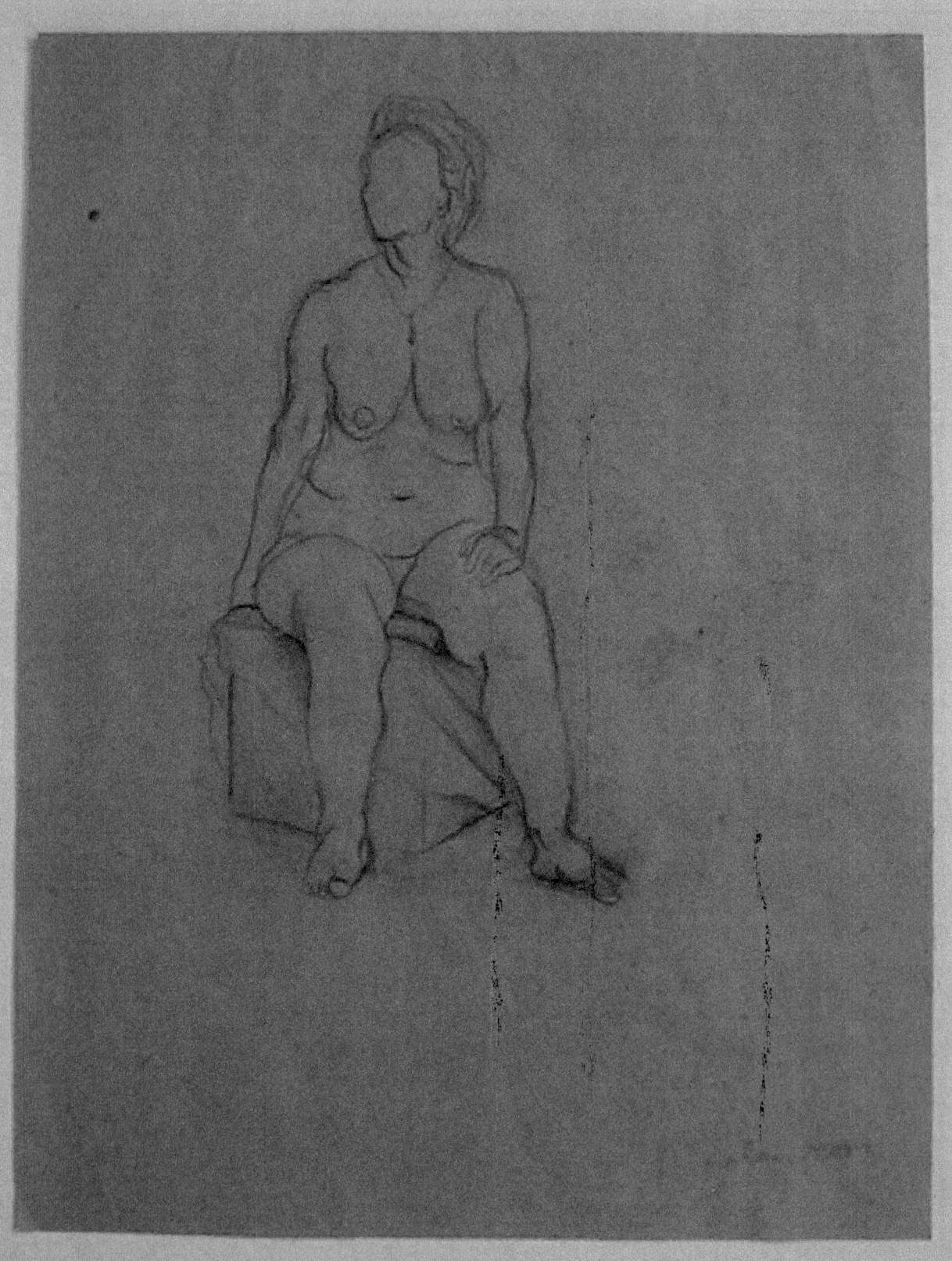

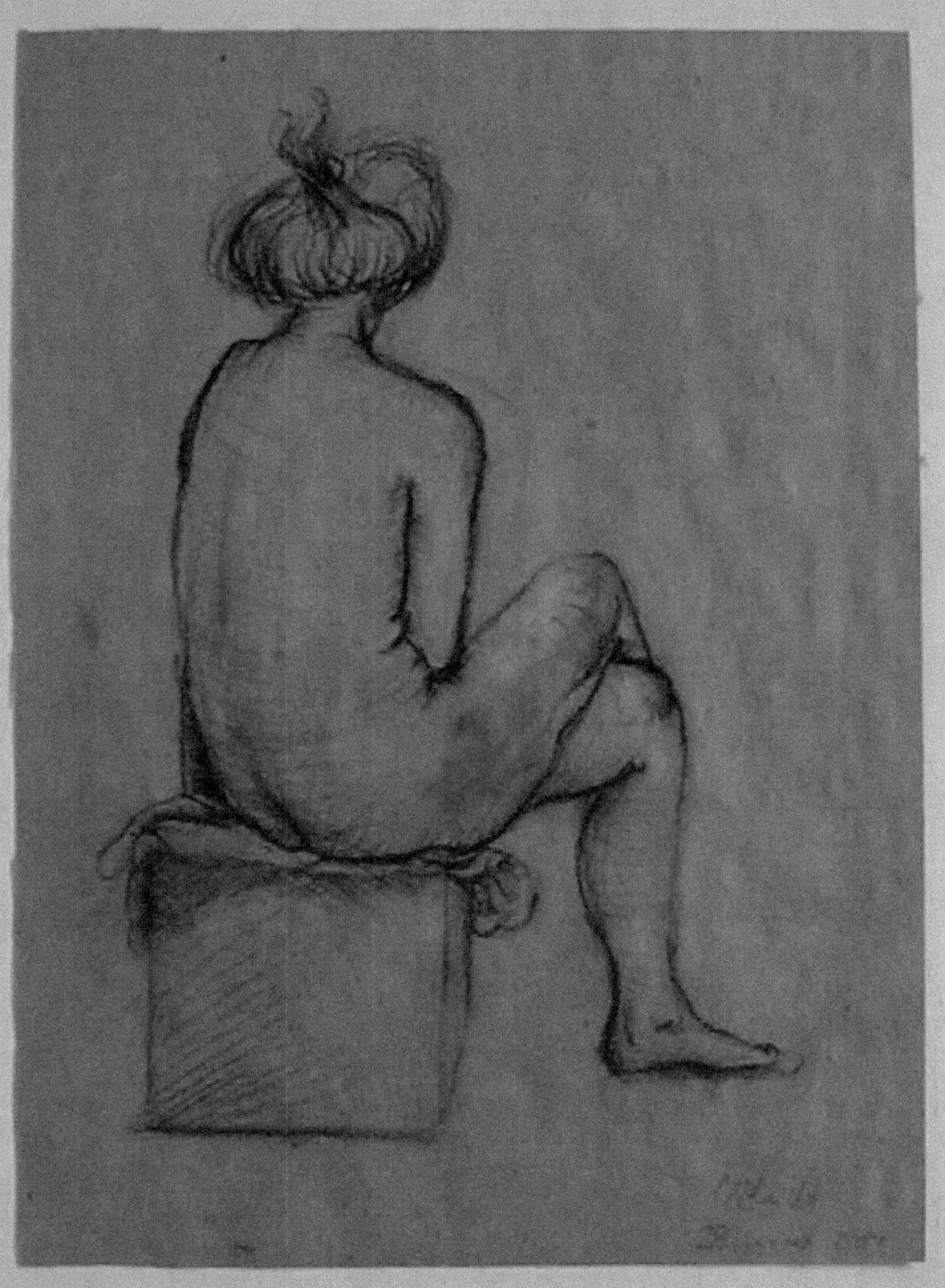

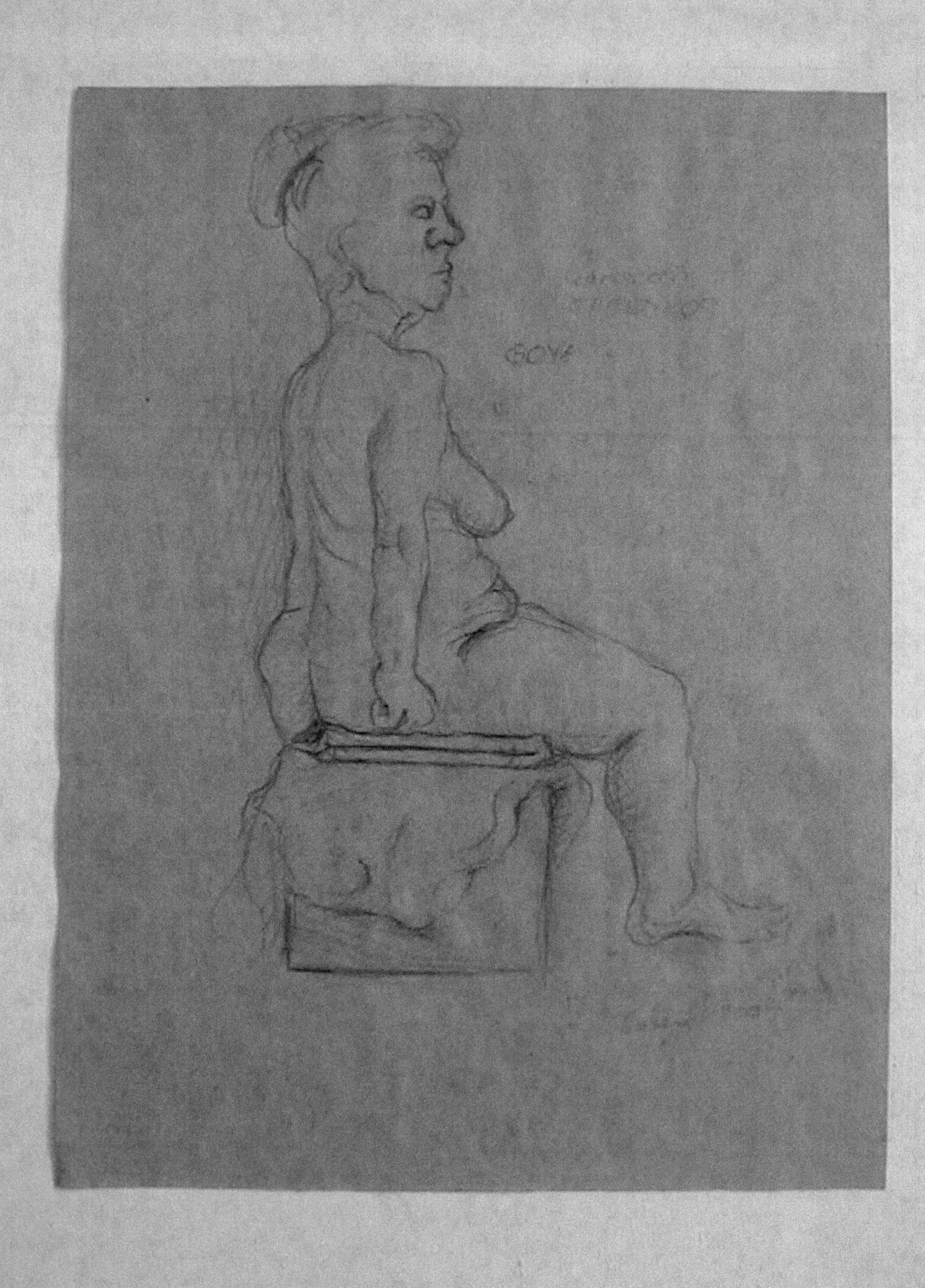

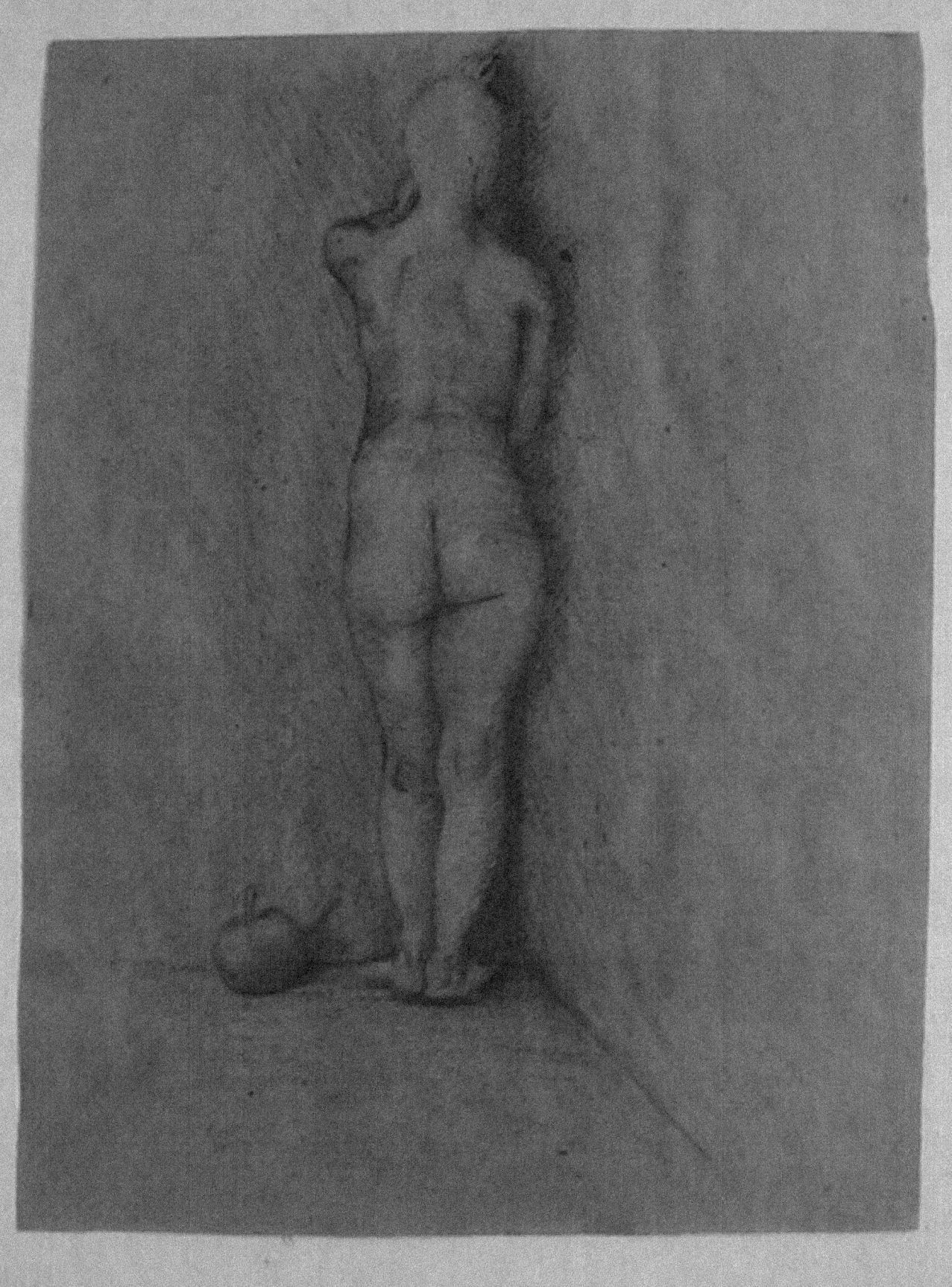

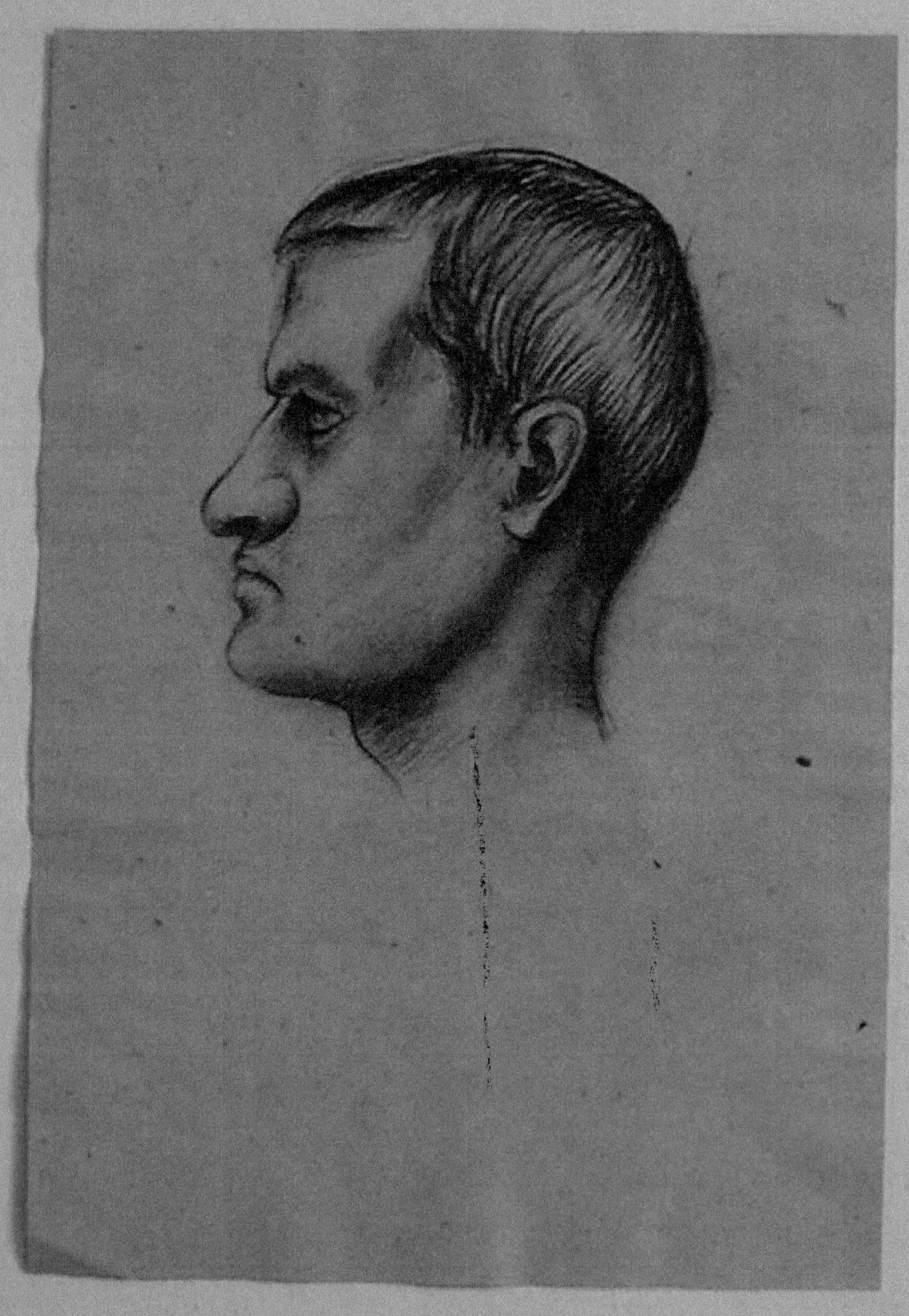

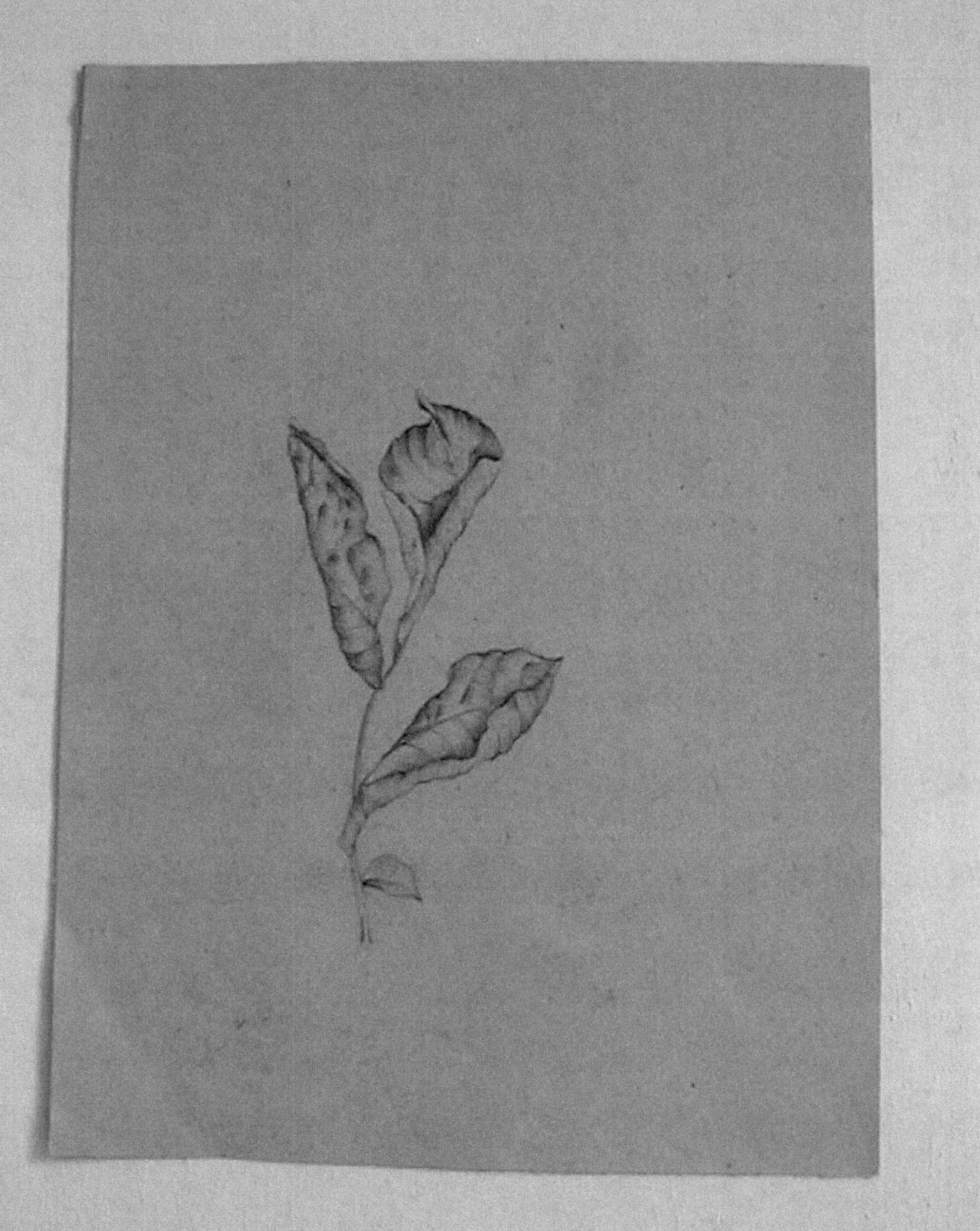

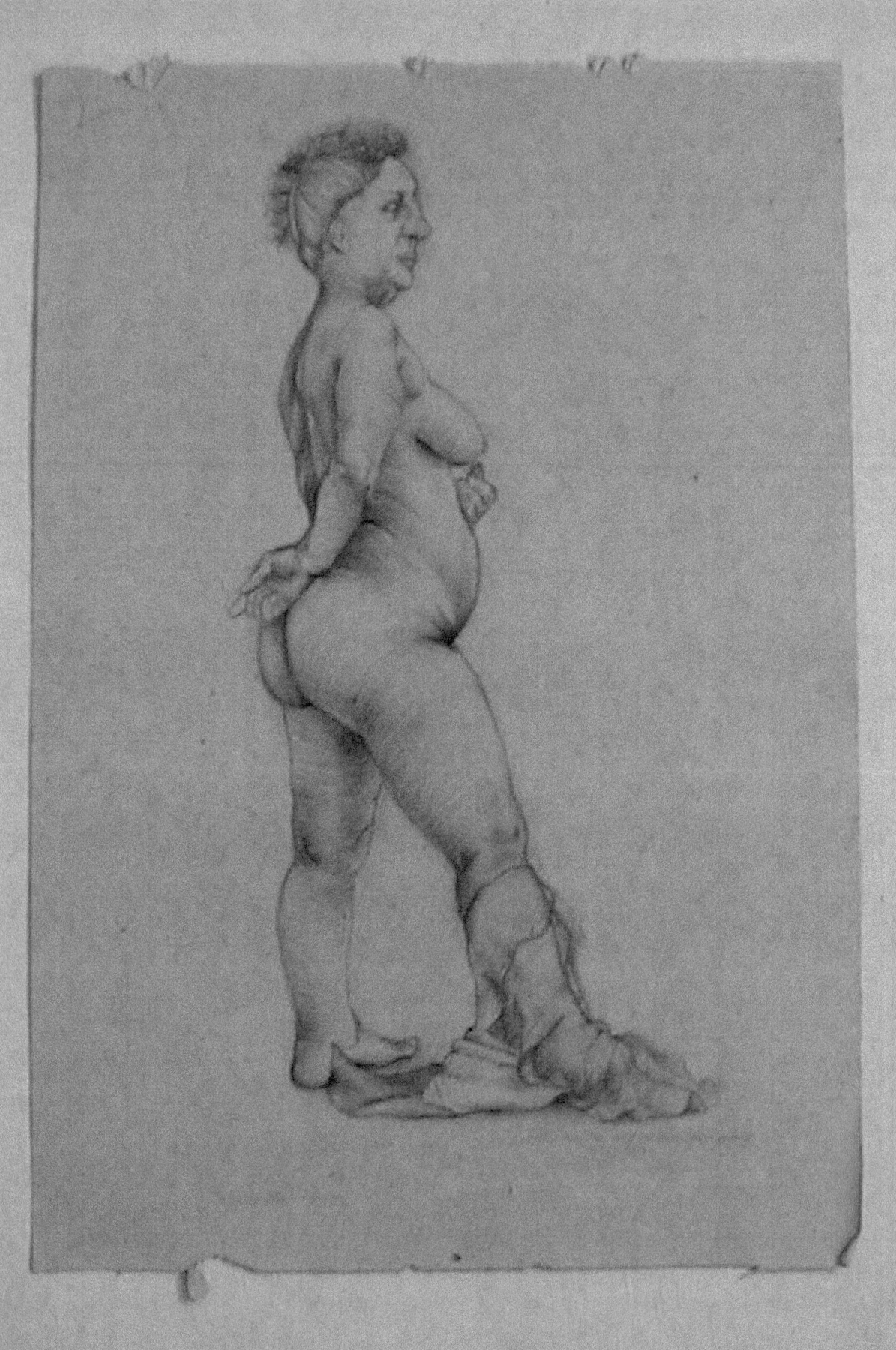

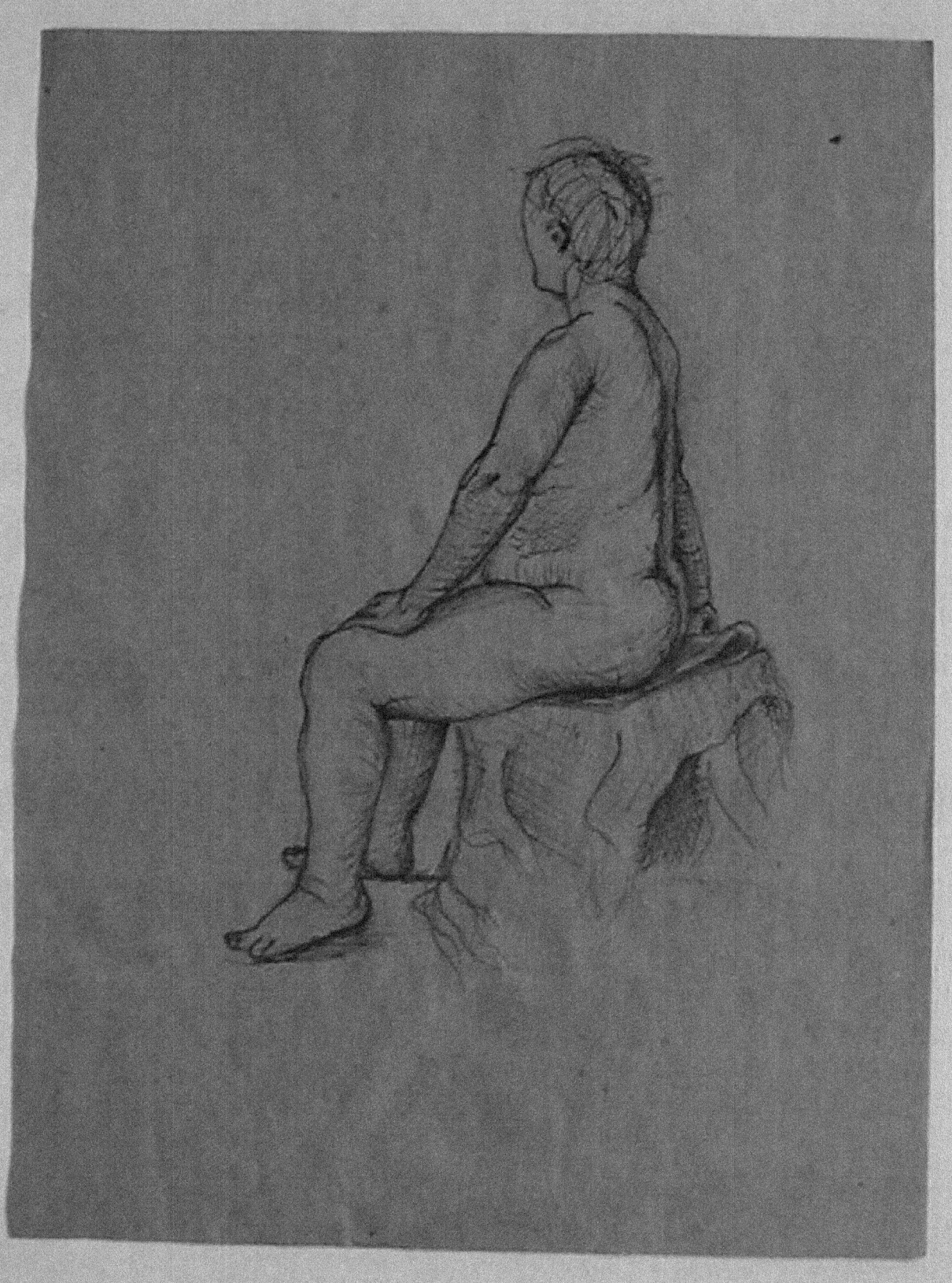

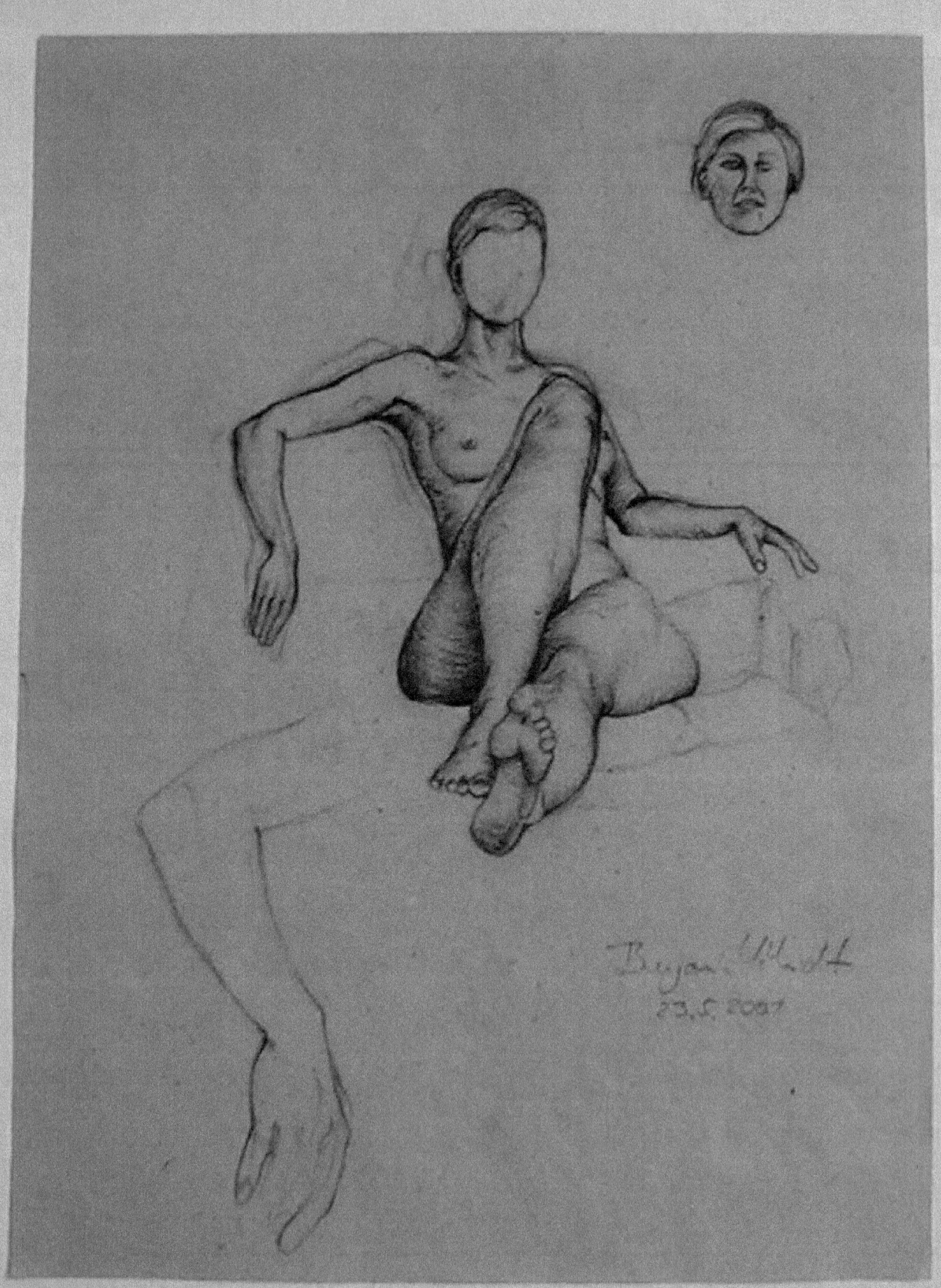

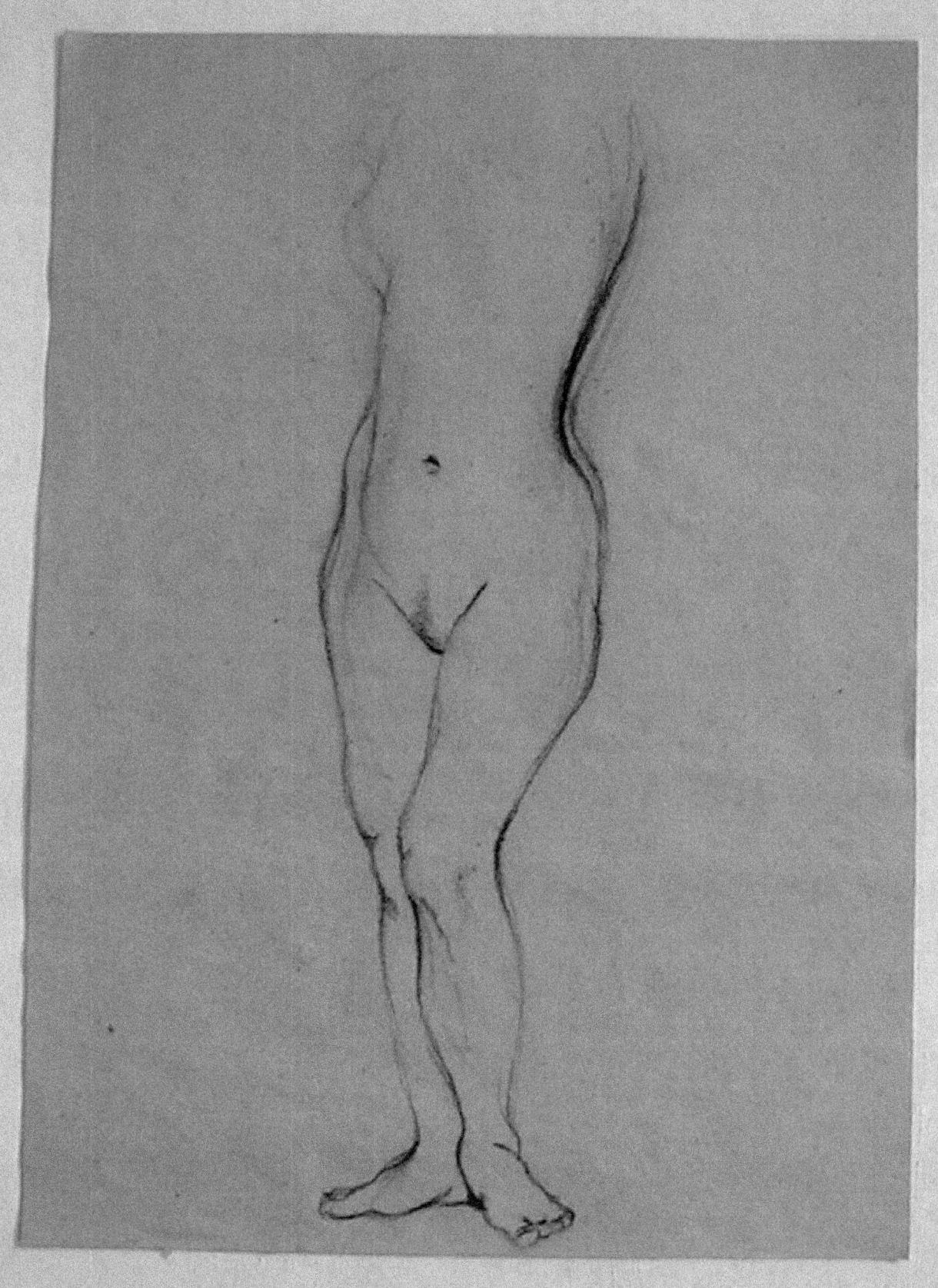

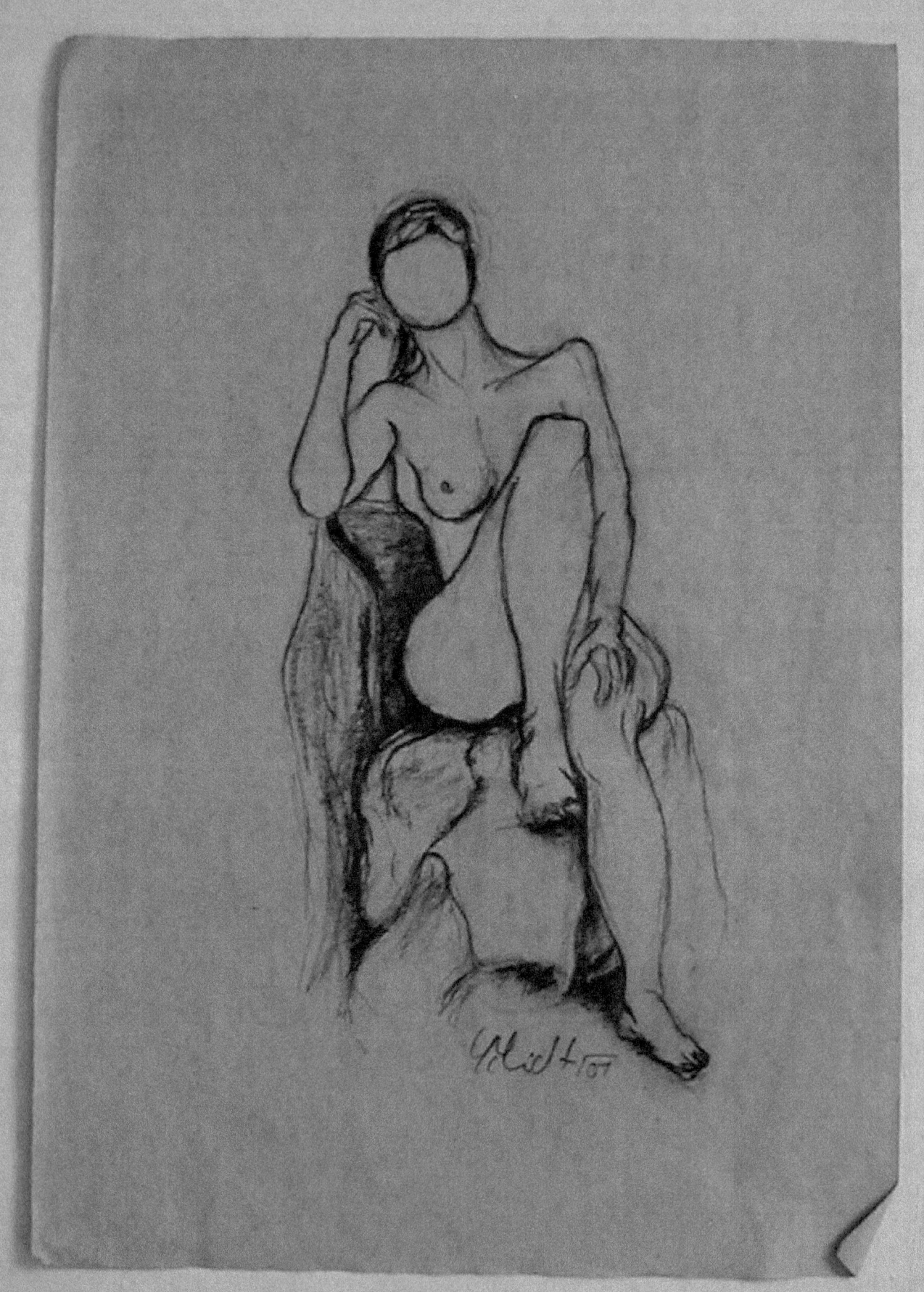

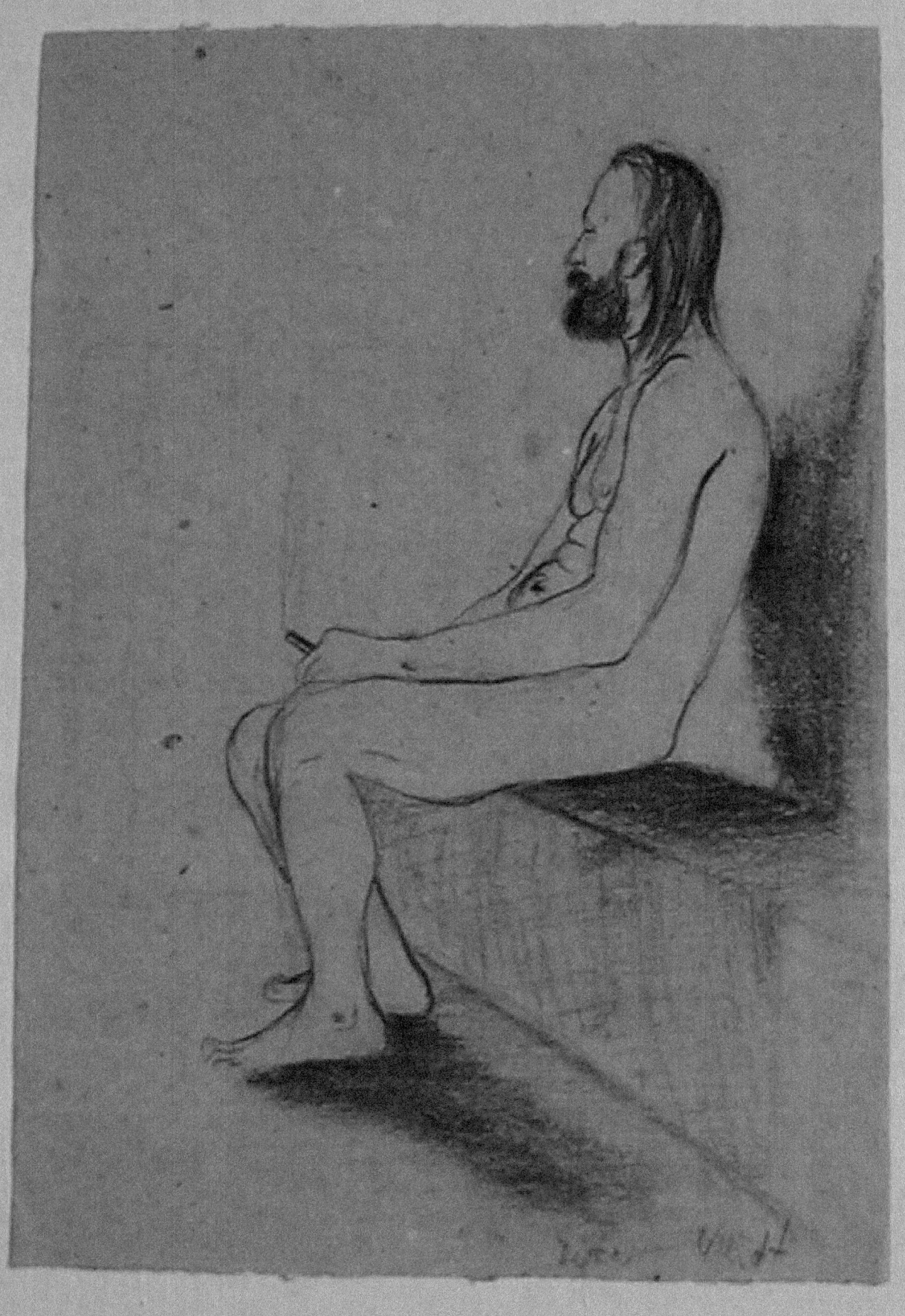

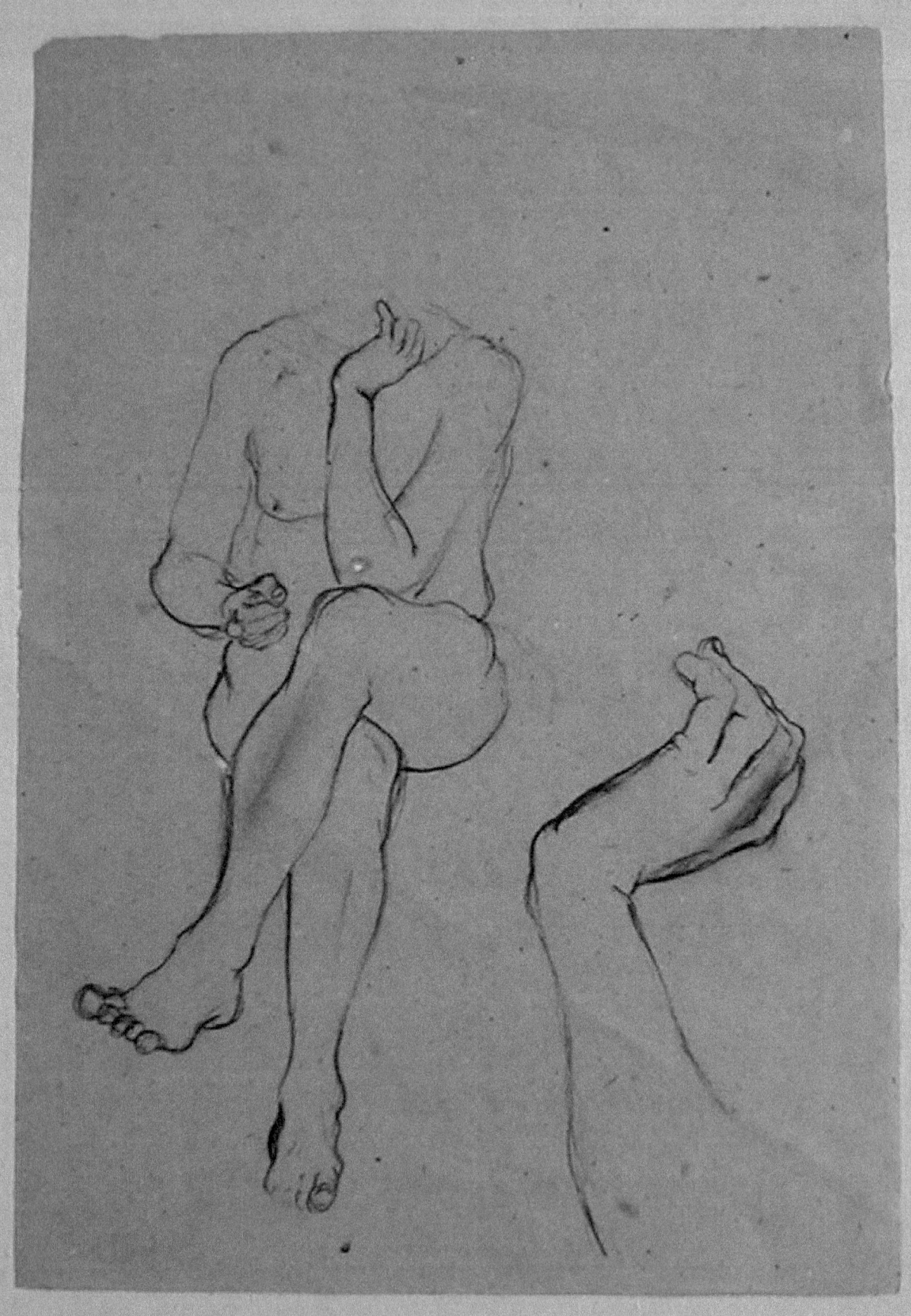

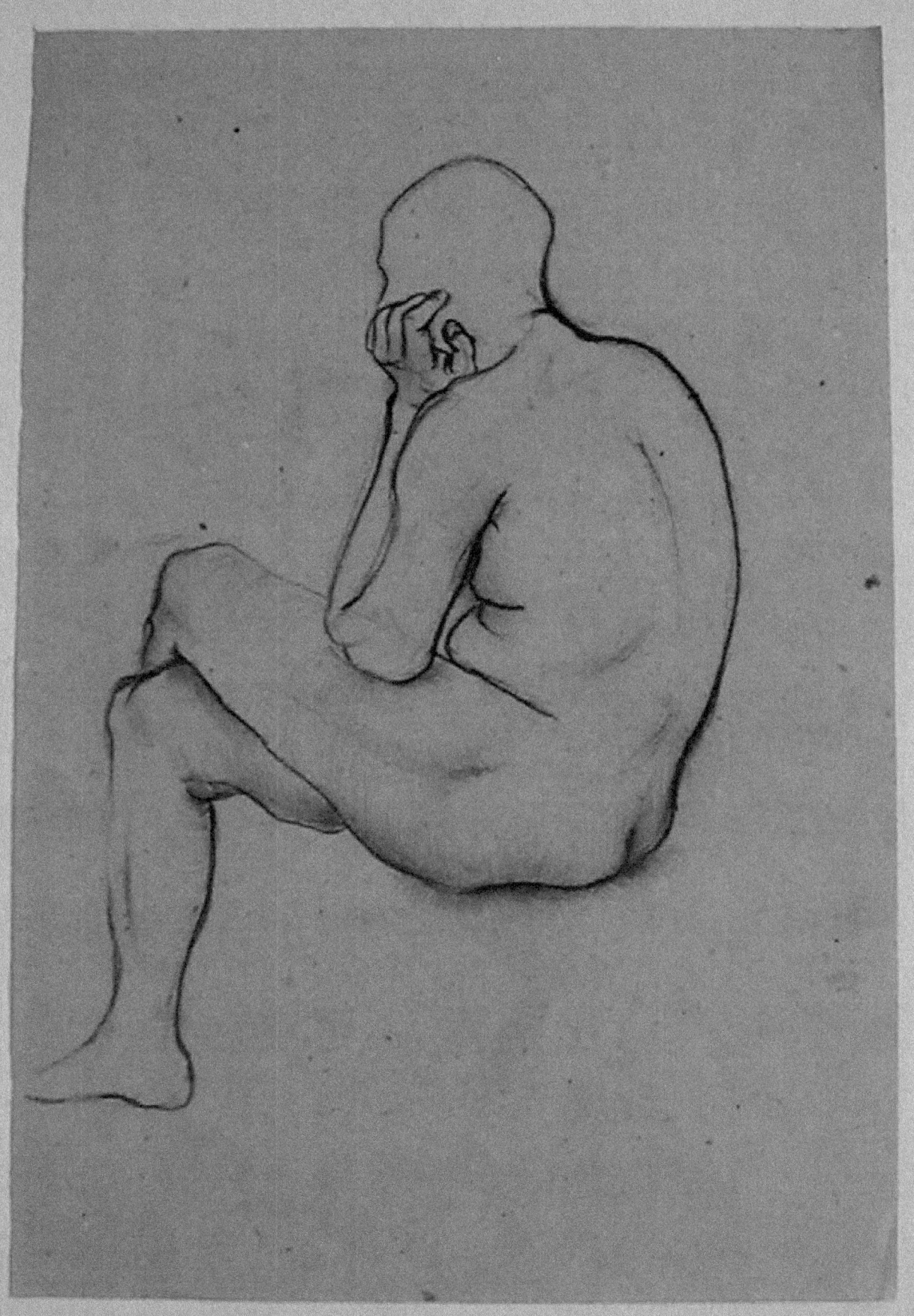

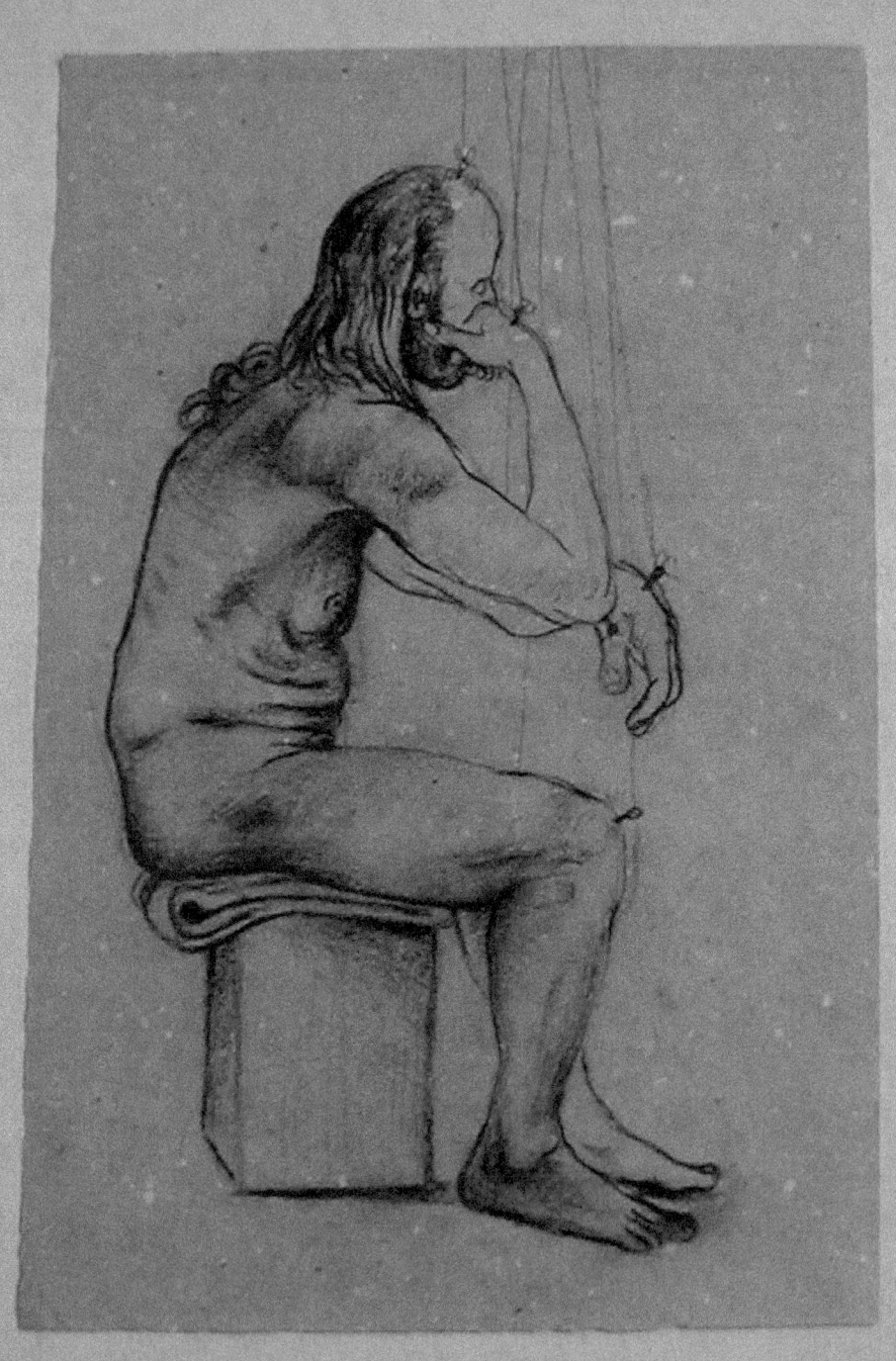

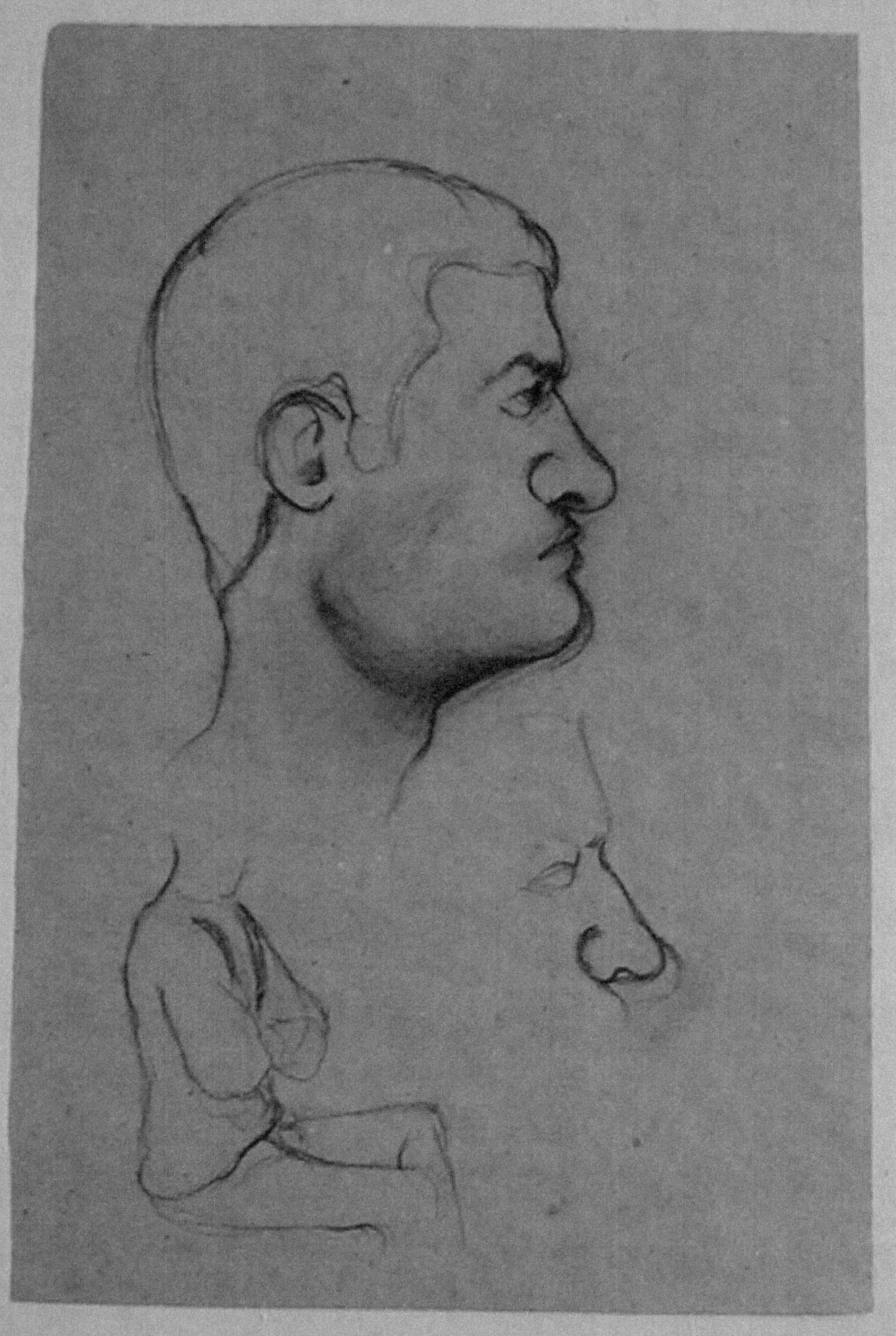

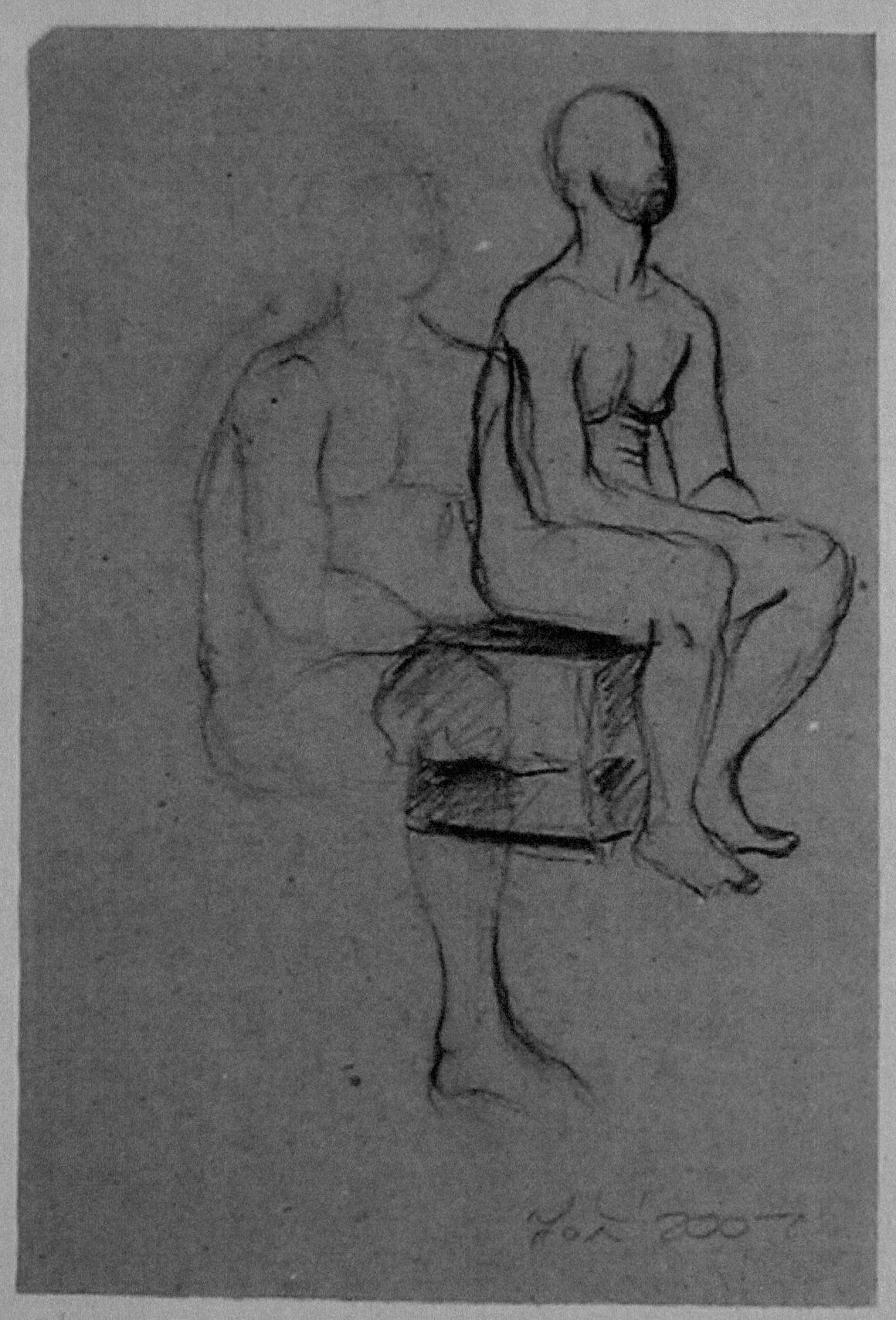

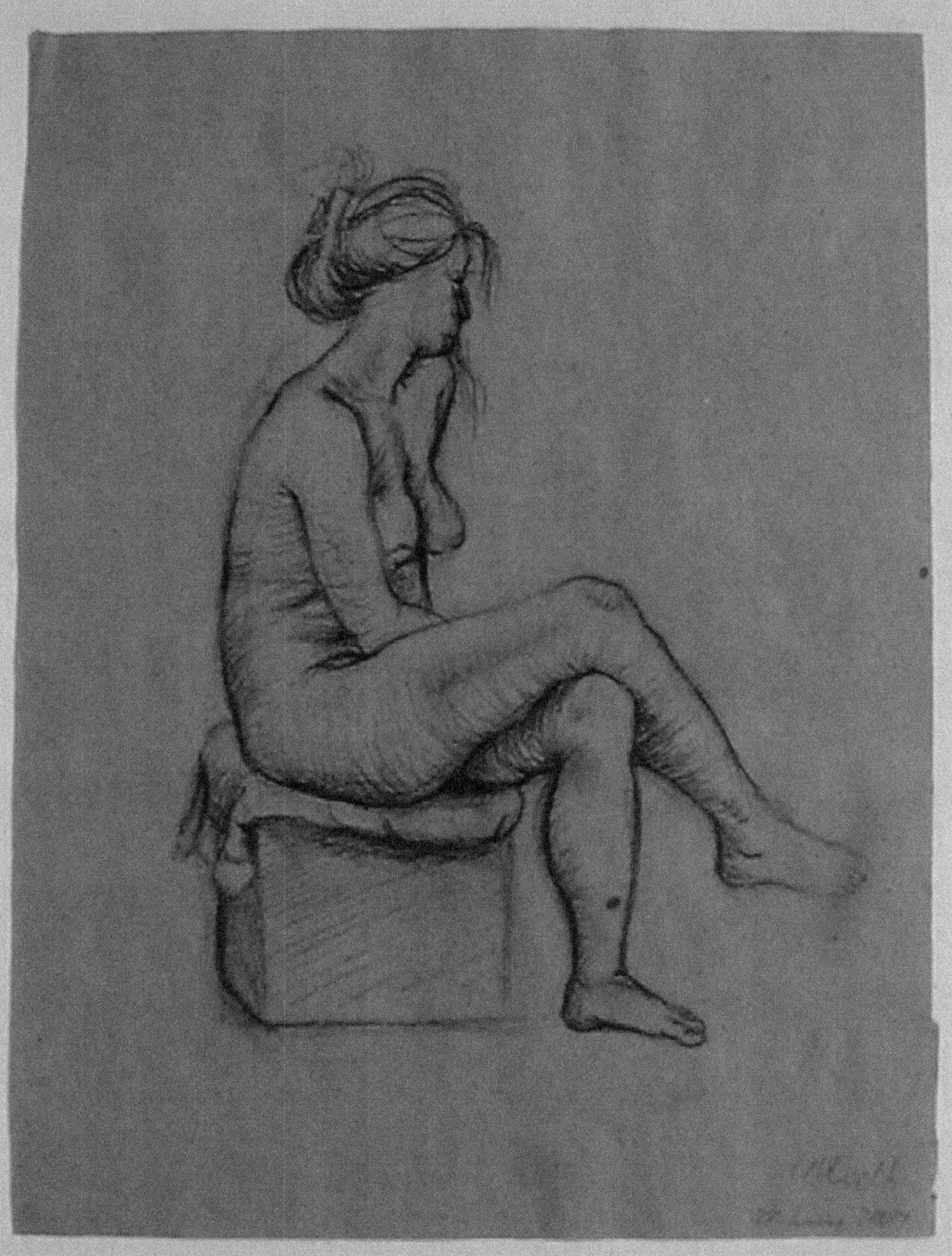

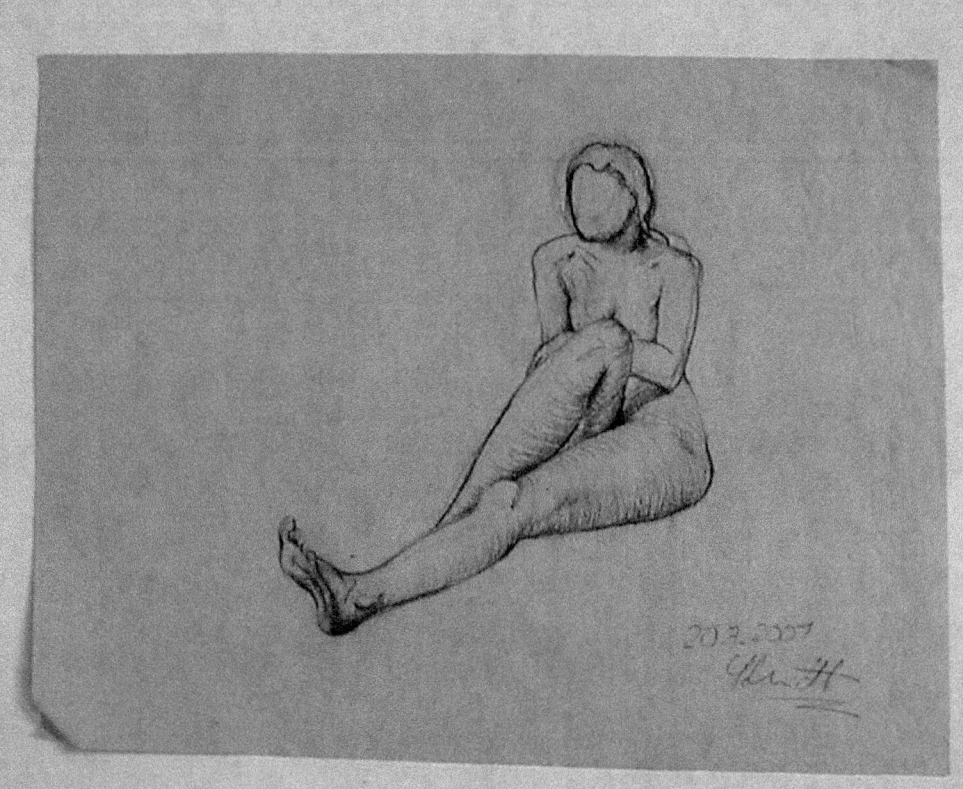

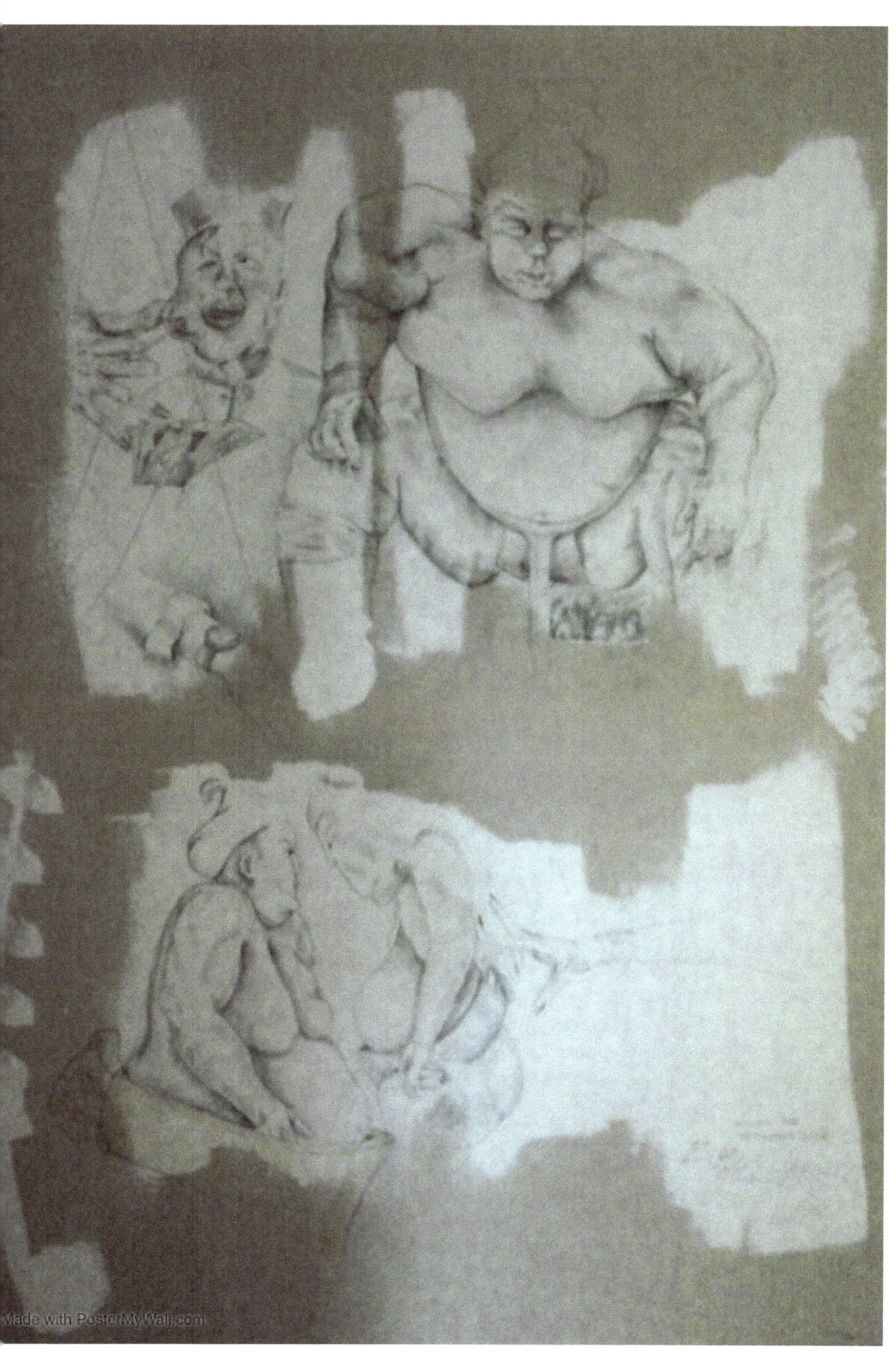
Made with PosterMyWall.com

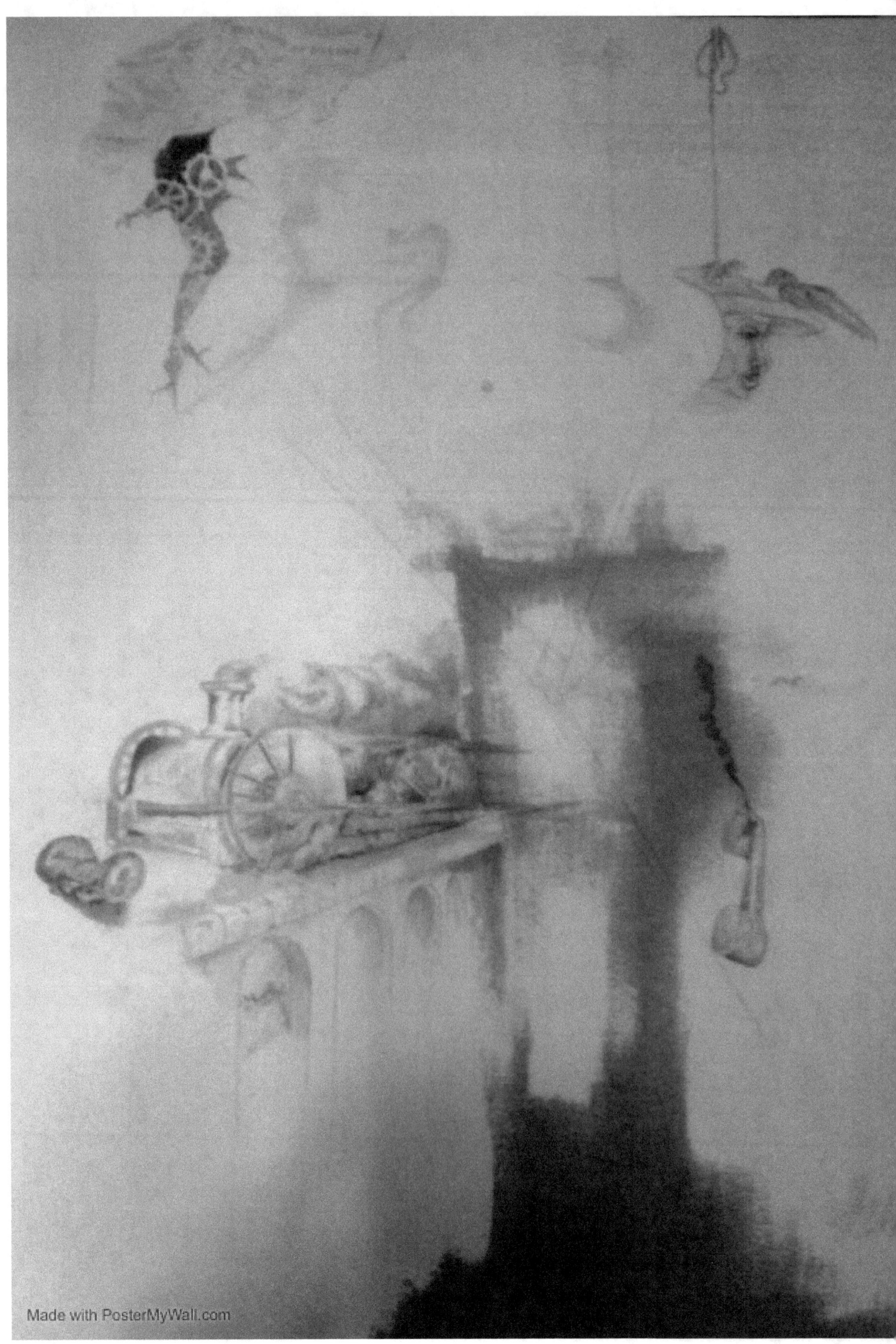

Made with PosterMyWall.com

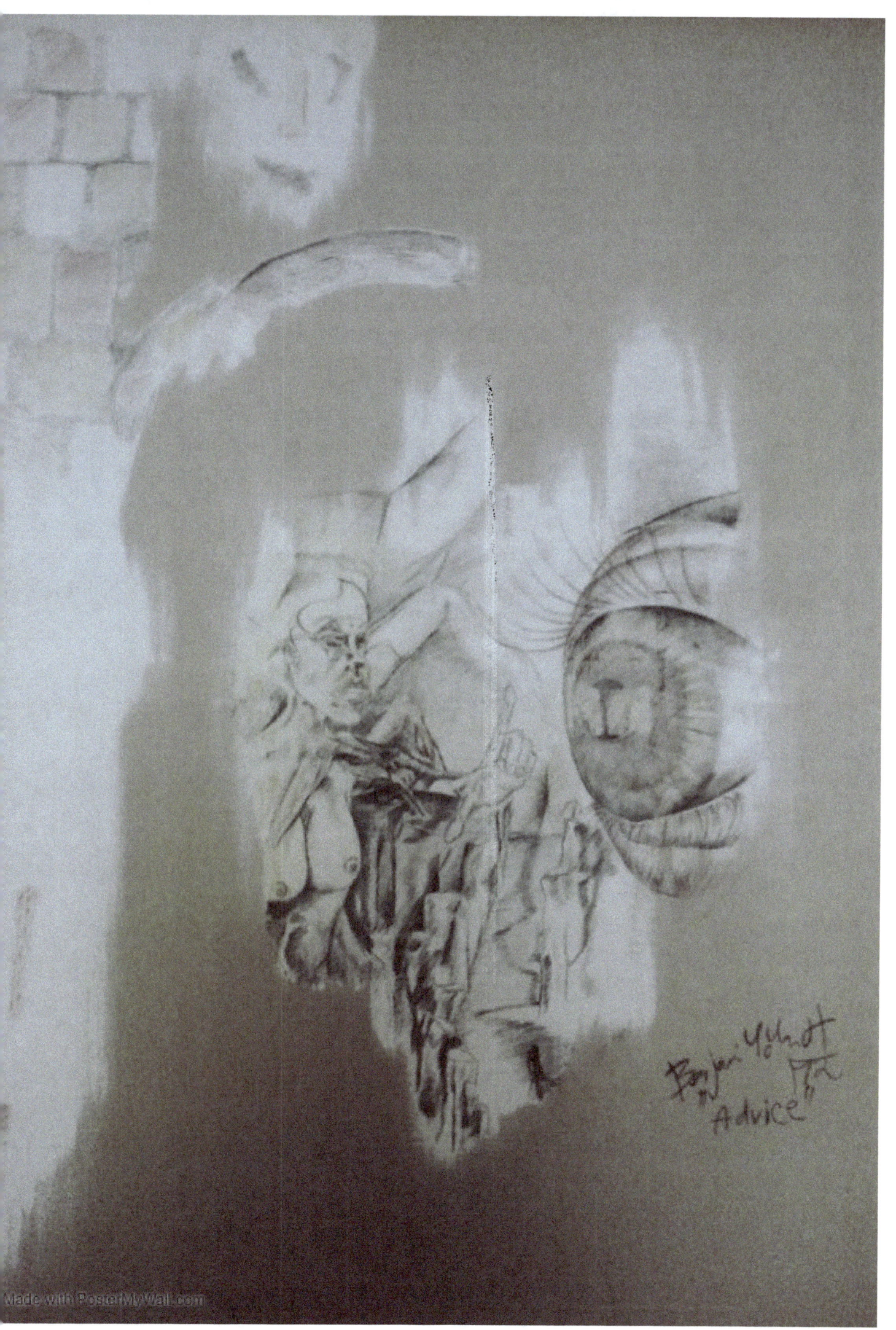
Made with PosterMyWall.com

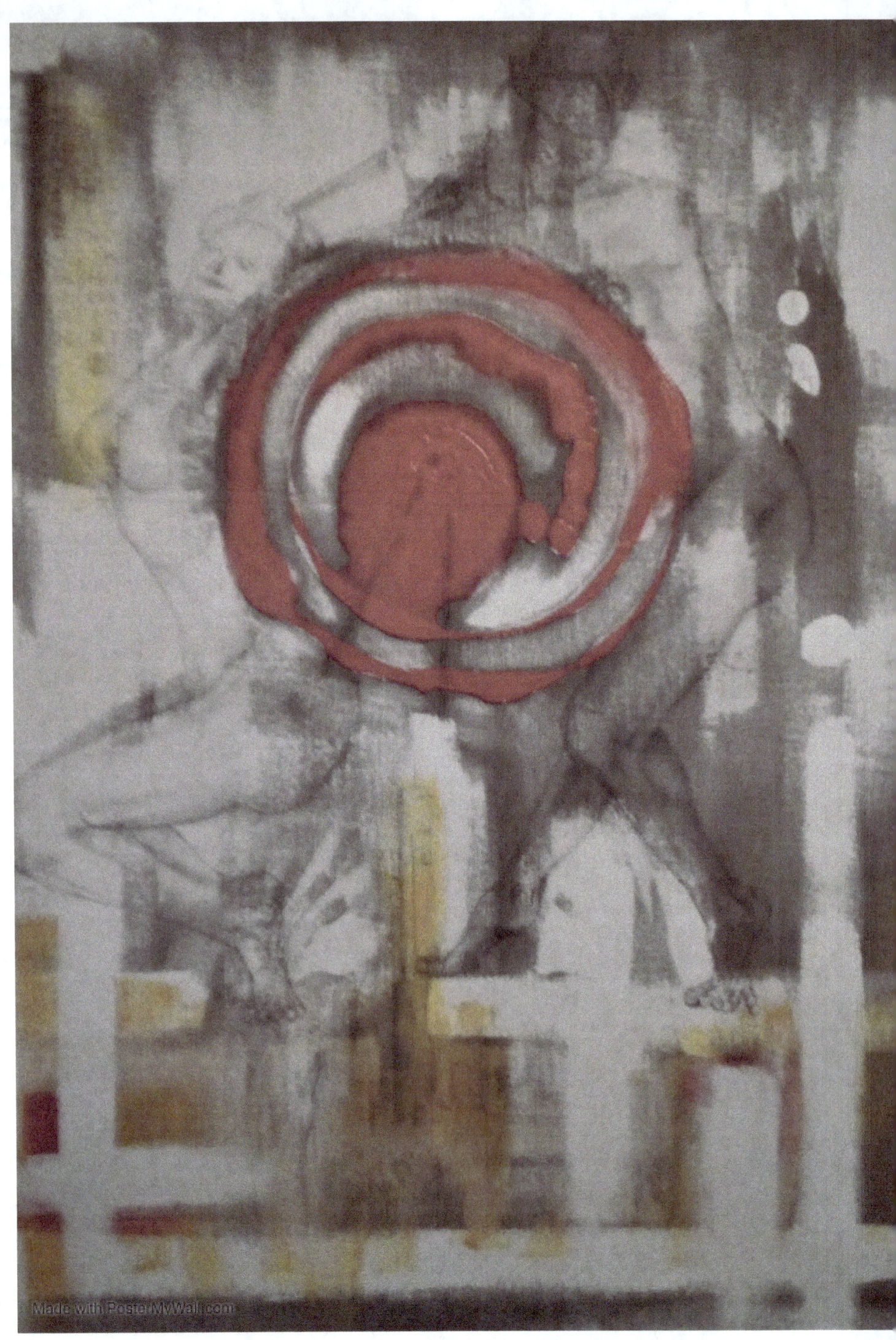
Made with PosterMyWall.com

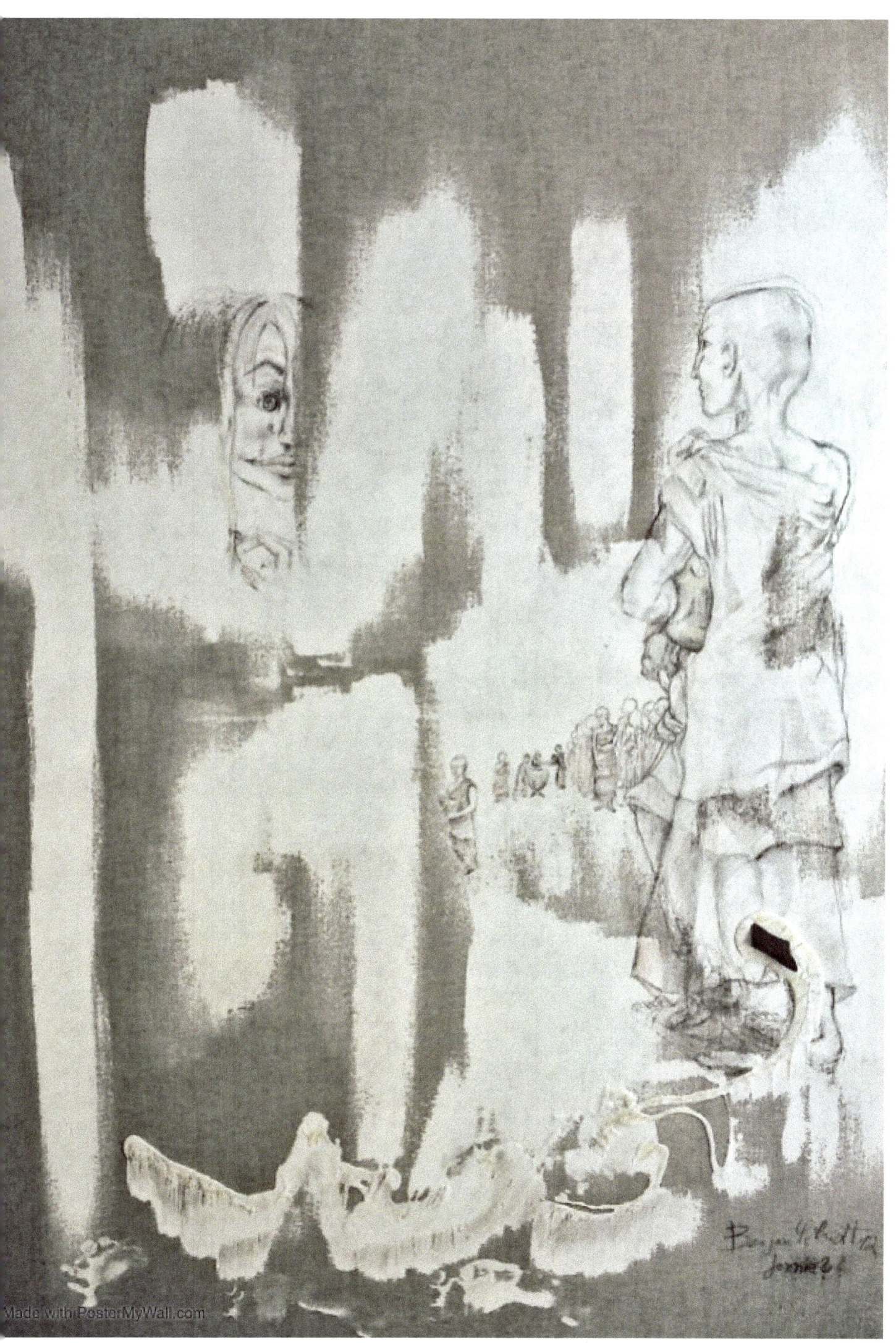
Made with PosterMyWall.com

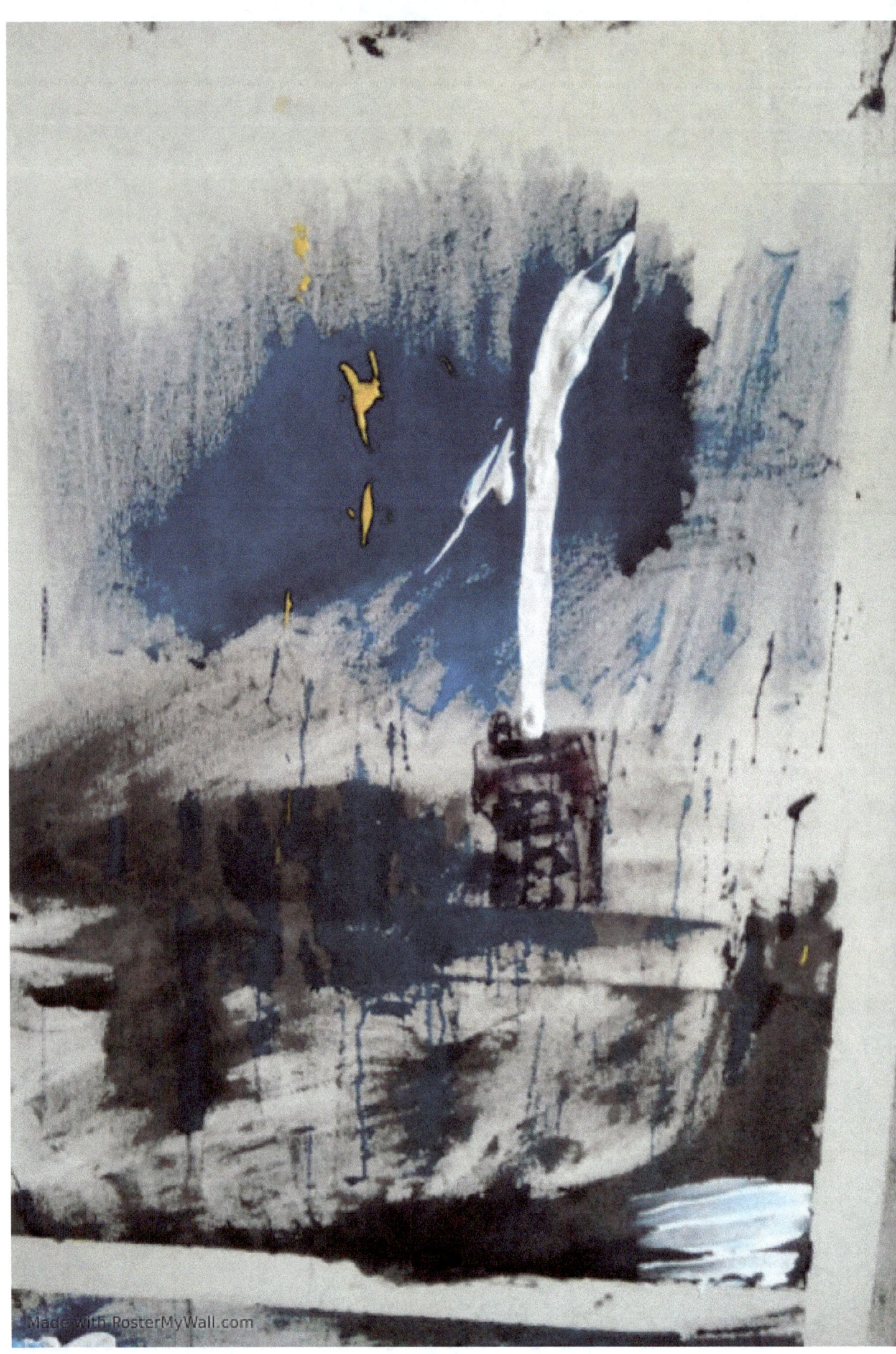
Made with PosterMyWall.com

www.ingramcontent.com/pod-product-compliance
Lightning Source LLC
Chambersburg PA
CBHW081057170526
45166CB00006B/2091